BUTLINS
Out Of The Dark And
Into The Light

by

Mathew Goody

This book is dedicated to my mum!

She never gave up on me and always gave me the strength to be a better person.

Although she is no longer with us, her memory will live On, and I will do my best to live up to being the Man she knew I would be.

Also, to all those who came before me and helped

Pave the way for people like me. I wouldn't Have known the friends and family I have Without you first showing us the way!

Butlins gave me the tools to be a better man

A better friend and gave me a home where I could feel safe and loved,

Thank you to you all!

ABOUT THE BOOK

This book began as a behind-the-scenes look at working at Butlins — a glimpse into the friendships that became family. But like a tree, the story grew, branching into moments both entertaining and serious. There were dark days, but my Butlins family pulled me through. The best part? Every word is true. It may be hard to believe, so sit back and experience the ride.

ABOUT THE AUTHOR

Some know Mathew as a friend, a few as family, but to most, he is a stranger. Yet, he has a story to tell — one that just might save lives. His journey has been extraordinary, and now is the time to share it.

Contents

Part 2

Chapter 43

Work was hard to come by; I was in for a long wait. It was getting me down, so I made a dramatic decision: one Sunday, I went to church. The same church I got married in. I wouldn't say I found God, but I did find peace. I was more lost than I realised, and just having that anchor every Sunday was what I needed.

Since the end of my marriage, I had a hole inside me that never seemed to get filled, and although I'd had relations since, nothing seemed to work. So, when I started going to church, I felt better. It was a long road ahead, and with the support of those around me, I knew I'd find my way again.

With that came the first glimmer of work. I got a call from someone I worked with at a hotel in my hometown; it had been taken over, and they were new to running a bar. I was asked if I would go in once a week to train them on how to clean the pipes. There is irony there, when it went pear-shaped in Crawley. Also, they needed someone to cook the full English breakfast on weekends. For me, that was a piece of cake and would at least keep me busy until a proper job came up.

Call it fate or just dumb luck, but in August 2008, I had an interview. We had a cinema being built and they were after staff;

of course, I went for it. It was held at the job centre and was in big groups — definitely a different style of interview, that's for sure. Thankfully, I got a job, just not the job I'd hoped for. This would become an issue down the line, and I would be pushed to my limit once again.

They built a complex with the cinema in the town centre. I applied to be a supervisor or higher but had to accept team member. The frustrating part was I had much more experience than the others applying. It was made worse as one of the new managers ran a bar in a nightclub, but as she knew the manager of another Cineworld, she got a manager's role straight away. The old 'it's not what you know, but who you know' was true.

The training was straightforward, and I was confident I could do the job. The one good thing was I love movies, so it was a perfect job — on the outside, at least — but favouritism was rife and couldn't be ignored.

The Friday we opened, we had a guest radio DJ — the one and only Pat Sharp — who broadcasted live from the cinema. Unfortunately, I had a hospital appointment that day, so didn't start until the Saturday morning. I thought I was ready, but I was very wrong — it was bedlam. They had 3 movies for juniors, which was 3 different child-friendly movies, and everyone brought their own food and drink. You wouldn't believe the mess that was left behind, and we only had 15 minutes to get in there and clean and tidy it up ready for the next showing.

We had 5 screens, the smallest having 120 seats and the biggest 365. You can imagine what it's like when they are full. Most people didn't take their rubbish with them. It certainly took some getting used to, to get them cleaned in the allotted time. Some staff would take the shortcut and push rubbish under the seats or just not make an effort. Some days I wondered why I bothered when others didn't, but I guess it's down to pride — not that anybody noticed.

After a month, five positions for temporary supervisor came up. I applied but was turned down — that was the first time. Two months later, the official positions came up. It coincided with me visiting my friend Christina in London. I had to have my interview over the phone. This was bad. I had based my interview on what I knew I could bring for the future of the company. In the end, it went to a Polish woman who had blonde hair, big bosom, and absolutely no experience in retail. That was the second time I dipped out.

Christmas and New Year 2008 was the last real fun I'd have working there, and as 2009 arrived, my health would once again become the bane of my existence. February 2009, I was booked in to have my bunion operated on. I was told it was one of the most painful operations you can have — they weren't wrong. It was also the biggest operation I'd had at that point.

Just before my six-week lay-up, one of the supervisors left and their position was up for grabs. Bad timing, to say the least. The manager said the job was mine as long as nobody else went for it. That was the worst thing he could have said. I needed the operation and couldn't afford to postpone it for a promotion. One person went for it while I was off and was given the role. He was another of the youngsters who was very good at doing as little as possible. That was the third time I was denied — you can see where this is going.

A bunion is a bony lump that appears behind the big toe on the side of the foot, and to rectify it means breaking the bone and realigning it, shaving bone off the edge of the bunion, and then adding two screws to the bone to help it heal. Having flat feet did not help the recovery.

The operation was a few hours long and was the best sleep I'd had in months — until the anaesthetic wore off. I quickly needed pain medication. It was like my foot was on fire and there was nothing I could do about it. They gave me morphine through a drip, and after a couple of minutes, it became more of a dull ache. The relief wouldn't last long; it was a constant battle that first day and night before becoming bearable.

It was the first time I'd spent a night in hospital since I was seven years old. I was there two nights. They had me standing an hour after being back on the ward. I had a special boot on the operated foot to protect it; I was told to keep the foot elevated for two weeks and keep the boot on for four more weeks after.

The hospital stay wasn't pleasant. It's hard being on hospital food when you are unable to eat most of it. I ended up living on dry toast and strawberry jelly.

There was a funny moment! I wasn't allowed to go to the toilet, so had to use one of their cartons — yes, those horrible things. I couldn't go lying down, so a male nurse helped me stand. One thing about being under anaesthetic — it makes your mind work differently. I knew I needed to go, but my body wouldn't let me. This equalled sign of possession. Yes, I was practically growling and scared the male nurse so much he couldn't get away from me fast enough.

I was glad to get back to my own bed. Two nights in hospital was too long. It was three weeks later I got the call the supervisor job had gone. I wasn't best pleased. I'd been with the company six months and three times denied the role I was more than capable of! I felt as though someone was laughing at my expense. It got to me and hit the depression hard. I was finding myself isolated from the rest of the staff. I was 30, and most were either much younger or much older. I was the odd one out. Those six weeks off at least gave me time to escape the crap.

The next few months went by with little to get excited about. I just got on with my job and tried to make the best of it. I still went to church; it was my safe place.

Although at times I felt like a hypocrite, I didn't believe in God! I'm a realist after all, and if religion had only been around 2,000 years, then how come our planet has been alive for billions of years? That's just my opinion. I never held it against anyone who believed — we all need something. At least at church I could be whoever I wanted to be. I wasn't judged and was always respected. I tried to get involved with different events they held, even singing a duet with another gentleman. I did make some friends. Christmastime was always good fun, singing Christmas carols. But after what happened November 2005, I no longer celebrated Christmas. I would put on a brave face for others. I got good at faking a smile that time of year. My mum saw right through me. Sadly, to this day, I still find no joy in Christmas. I came close in 2013. All will become clear.

Then it was 2010. It's true when they say the years go quicker the older you get. This would be one of the hardest years I'd ever experienced. *Avatar*, the movie, had just come out at the cinema. I really wanted to see it in 3D, but that meant going out of town. I'd planned to go to Cambridge to see it with someone I worked with. 7th January would be the day that changed everything. Winter had been a hard one. We had a lot of snow New Year's Eve, and although by the 7th the snow had gone, there was a lot of ice around. I had a fear of slipping over. I purposely walked slowly to avoid a fall. This was a mistake.

I had just left my parents' house on my way to our bus station. I was excited I was finally going to see a 3D movie. I'd already seen it twice in 2D and loved the film. I knew the 3D would be amazing. For a moment, I wasn't paying enough attention to the path I was walking on. Around 30 metres from my parents' home, one second I was on my feet, and the next I wasn't. Time stood still — one leg then the other went up in the air. I hit the ground hard as I landed flat on my back.

It was very reminiscent of Butlins when I slipped over while carrying a tray, but this time it was much, much worse. The ice is unforgiving and takes no prisoners. Boy, did it hurt. The shock just about kept the pain from hitting me full on. After a couple of minutes, I managed to pick myself up and check for any signs of injury. I felt lucky — it could have been worse. Least, that's what I thought. My back hurt, but it was bearable. After five minutes of standing there, I decided to still go to Cambridge.

The journey took an hour. I had a niggling in the base of my back but was too determined to see a 3D movie. It wasn't the best decision when the film is nearly three hours long. Somehow, I managed to get through it and was glad I went. My body didn't agree with my mind. The journey home was harder, and the pain kicked up a notch — not enough to make me cry out, but enough to remind me that something was wrong. That night wasn't any better, but I was so exhausted I managed to sleep.

The next morning, I was in more pain. My back was throbbing. I knew then it was worse than I thought. I immediately called my doctors for an appointment. It would be later that day I got seen. After a check-over, it was obvious it needed further investigation. They sent me for an X-ray and signed me off work for a week.

When the results came in, they told me there was a big problem! They immediately referred me to see a neurologist. I didn't know what would happen, but I hoped I'd get some answers and get back to work.

When I first saw the consultant, he checked my back's flexibility. The discomfort was obvious and he decided to send me for an MRI scan. While this was going on, I was signed off work. The pain got so bad I struggled to do anything most days. I felt like my whole life was on hold with no sign of ending!

My boss at work wanted to have regular meetings to see how I was doing and see if they could help. I'm sure it was to see if I was genuine or just pulling a fast one. It would be the only time I had respect for my manager. He told me he could see how much pain I was in as I kept flinching and couldn't sit still. The manager told me he had back problems in the past and knew what I was going through. I doubt that he suffered as much as I did. One good thing — he gave me permission to use the cinema. At first, I would go regularly until the pain got worse. I could see some of the staff giving me looks as though they didn't believe I was genuine.

The MRI results turned my world upside down! I had an L5 S1 slip; it was serious. The second vertebra up from the base of my spine had slipped out of position, and if it slipped further, I could end up paralysed from the waist down. This would include no ability to control my bowel, bladder, and no feelings below the waist. The best option was surgery, which would involve putting two rods and a number of screws against my spine, with a cage to help the bones heal. After the accidents and falls I'd had, surgery was my best option. I'd find out the foot surgery was a walk in the park compared to back surgery.

As the surgery got closer, my nerves and anxiety kicked in. I was terrified. They told me it was a big surgery and the risks involved included paralysis, the operation failing, and infection that could lead to further problems. There was a lot to process. I wouldn't have managed without the support of my mum and my Butlins friends. I still regularly talked to Phil, Louise, and Tracy. I was blessed having them in my life. Had my foot surgery failed, I would have been in more pain but it would have been bearable. If the back surgery failed, I may never walk again. I may never have the pleasure of being with a woman. All these scenarios went through my mind. It was horrible.

The morning of the surgery, I was at the hospital at 6:45 a.m. I tried to remain positive. Once I was on the ward, I found out I was first on the list. That was when they found out I had never had a pre-op appointment, so they had a panic on to get it done. While they did the checks, the surgeon came to see me to prepare me for what was going to happen, and then the anaesthetist. It was madness, as nobody wanted to start the day being behind.

When I woke up after the surgery, I was so thirsty. A few minutes later, the pain kicked in. I knew pain and believed I had a high threshold for it. I was wrong. It started as a niggly pain. It soon became the most intense I had ever suffered. I was petrified. No amount of warning or education on what to expect could have prepared me for the agony, and it never ended. I had a morphine drip that I could use every 10 minutes, which barely touched me. Then I tried to move — huge mistake. I couldn't lift my body an inch. The pain hit me like a tidal wave. It was a pain like no other. It was a scary time. Then I noticed I had a catheter. That was a first for me. I was grateful — there was no way I would be able to go to the toilet, and no chance I'd be walking any time soon.

They warned me it was a painful surgery, as they were working close to nerves in the spine and the spinal cord. I never knew how debilitating it would be. I was moved to a ward after being released from recovery. I tried to move, but every time I couldn't physically do it. I knew I wasn't paralysed, as I could feel my legs and wiggle my toes. I was beginning to wonder if it was worth it. They told me I would have a two-week recovery before being allowed back to work. I thought they were joking. I couldn't see how I would get over this that quickly, let alone be back working.

After midnight, I'd just dozed off when two nurses told me, due to an emergency, they were moving me to another ward. I was still out of it. I mumbled something. I didn't get much sleep — the pain was too much. I couldn't keep quiet and felt bad for the other patients hearing me groan.

The next morning, they brought me some food that I just about managed to eat, and then the nurse told me that I had to get out of bed. I laughed at her and asked if she was joking, and she said no and that I would have to come off the morphine. I thought she was being cruel, and even though she smiled at me, she was serious. I wondered if I was in Helga's house of horrors. No pain, no gain—no thanks. But somehow the worst of the pain had subsided to a dull ache, and finally, I was able to move again. It still hurt a lot, but I was no longer stuck on my back. It was 9:30 a.m., and the nurse stood over me as I struggled to sit up. I won't lie—it was horrible, but some women just won't be ignored.

Coming off the morphine was the worst. I argued to have it longer. I was told no, and I gave in. Somehow, I could stand. In the space of an hour, I went from a crippled man stuck in bed and on morphine to no morphine and, with help, able to put my two feet on the floor without falling over or feeling dizzy. Then came removing the catheter. I was nervous.

Having a small tube pulled out of your manhole was no fun, but not painful. It was definitely an eye-opener when you saw all the nastiness on the tube. It's easy to forget what is going on inside your body when you can't see it. It was a relief to have it out. I was shocked at how long the tube was. The nurse was very kind and put me at ease.

Although I was over the worst, I was still in hospital for another night. Most of the day, I was trying to get my stability back and exercise. The sooner I got back to normal, the sooner my body would heal. The pain levels had dropped significantly, but I still hurt.

I was able to get more sleep that night — until I had a repeat of the night before. I was moved to yet another ward, this time the geriatric ward. I felt like an old man, even though I wasn't the only younger person in there. I'd already seen the consultant, who told me he was very happy with the surgery and was hopeful I would have no lasting issues. I was going to find out the hard way that luck wasn't on my side.

The next morning, I was told I would be going home that day. I just needed the doctor to sign me off and to wait for a prescription. Anyone who's spent time in hospital knows waiting for a prescription is the thing that always holds up being released. I was glad when I called my parents with an idea of when I could go home. I was lucky that I was living with my parents and didn't have to recover on my own. When you go through something as dramatic and painful as that, knowing your mum is there to support you really does help.

Ten days after the surgery, I had my stitches out. That was when I got my first look at my back. It was done through keyhole, and I had five incisions. I thought that would make a nice dot-to-dot for someone one day. It's funny where your mind goes in the face of adversity. The next week was spent getting into a routine — to get ready for returning to work. Although I would only be working for one week, as I was booked in to have a second operation on my left foot after the bunion had returned.

Chapter 44

Being back for one week seemed pointless; nobody showed any concern after being off work for months. Just like that, I was back in hospital. I was recovering from the back surgery, but having more surgery so soon wasn't smart. Thankfully, the second foot surgery was easier than the first and I only had to stay in one night. I was able to get out of bed not long after reaching the ward. Knowing what to expect helped. The recovery was easier too. The hardest part was my foot itching, until the stitches came out. I was in for a busy couple of years with more surgery planned. There is only so much you can put your body through before you get tired.

I returned to work and all was the same. I did get the nickname the 'oracle' of Cineworld. I tried to watch all the movies that we showed so I would know what the regulars would like. When you see the same people week in, week out, you get a sense of what they like, and then they would ask me to recommend a film. Most of the time, I got it spot on. One of my many talents.

I survived another month before the problems started. My back was bad and I knew it. It started with an aching pain in my lower back which progressed to my right leg. I didn't think it would last, so tried to ignore it. I had my follow-up appointment with the consultant and raised my concerns. I had fresh X-rays to see how my back was healing.

The X-rays looked good, but the consultant could see something wasn't right. It took some back and forth before he decided on a nerve root block. He said the cage that was in my back may have been sitting on the nerve that ran down my right leg. The nerve root block would, in theory, numb the nerve. At that point, I was desperate for anything to stop the pain. February 2011, I had the nerve root block — to me, it was make or break. I didn't fancy having another surgery, and if it didn't work, then that was definitely a possibility. After what I went through the first time, I wasn't too keen.

It was done under CT. There were three people in the room. I was told to lie on my front while they performed the procedure. I felt the injection straight away; it started in my back and went down my leg to my foot. It wasn't nice and drained me. It took about 10 minutes but felt much longer. Afterwards, the assistant told me to take as long as I needed before leaving. I was grateful, as I had rubber legs. After a few minutes trying to gather myself, another person came in and told me to hurry up and leave. I felt pressured, so leave I did. Only problem was, I was moving like a drunk and couldn't control my legs. They let me leave, stumbling, and I had to hang on to the wall to stop myself falling over. It wasn't pretty, but I managed to make it out of the hospital and just about reached the bus stop. It was a huge relief when I got home. I spent the rest of that day crashed out.

The next couple of months were horrible. My right leg was getting worse to the point I couldn't stand for longer than an hour at a time. I had a follow-up with the consultant and he told me if the nerve root block had worked, he would have operated again to remove the cage. But because I was suffering so much and had no quality of life, he agreed another operation was the only option.

Before I had it, I would end up going in for knee surgery. I already had multiple issues with my knees; the back made them worse. The knee X-rays and MRIs showed no problems, but the consultant said there was clearly something wrong and agreed on exploratory surgery. He found the material behind the knee-cap was rubbing and causing a lot of discomfort. The surgery was a success — until I woke up and the pain started. I was practically bouncing on the bed while in tears from the pain. It was day surgery, and I couldn't leave until the pain was under control. It made for a long day. I was beginning to wonder if I was going to be forever cursed after each surgery.

My second back operation was on the 29th November 2011! They said they would need to do open surgery but I should be able to go home the following day. I was reserved on that but hoped all the same. When I woke up afterwards, I was surprised to find the pain levels were nowhere near as bad as the first operation. That was a good sign, and although I still needed pain medication, it was much less than the previous one. They put me in a side room on my own after leaving recovery. This was because after my first back operation, they got the results back from the pre-op and found I had MRSA — a superbug that, if not treated, can turn to MRSI and be very dangerous. Although I'd had the treatment after the diagnosis, they put me down as a carrier, so I had to be in a side ward.

Within half an hour, I was walking around — quite the contrast to the last time. I believed open surgery was more demanding on the body and would require longer to heal, but I was wrong. They had used one of the entry points from the keyhole surgery, so I've now got four little scars and one big one. It isn't pretty and would take a long time to get used to. After one night in hospital, I was told I could go home if I felt well enough. To be honest, I just wanted to get outside and smoke — yes, bad habit, but it is my only real vice. As I was waiting on my release paperwork and prescription, one of the nurses asked me if I was leaving, which I told her yes. She then said it was a shame because she liked me. Typical — I thought she was beautiful and very kind. Ah well, I couldn't really say I've changed my mind, and I doubt anybody really enjoys staying in hospital.

By the time I had the second back operation, it was the sixth operation and one procedure in just over two years. It was a lot to go through and made recovery harder. I had youth on my side; that was the only saving grace. Another supervisor role came and went; the manager told me to go for it again before turning me down. I was getting frustrated and knew that favouritism was taking over the place. The Polish woman who'd made supervisor over me previously had left and returned to Poland for a few months, then decided to come back, and not only did she get a job back, she was given a manager's job. It was clear the boss had a thing for her. The fact that she was blonde with a big bosom probably helped. I ended up letting rip one day. I'd had enough of being taken advantage of when people with no experience and undeserving got promoted. The general manager kept stringing me along. I got taken into the office after that. They said it was out of character for me and hoped it didn't happen again. What made it worse was the Polish lady had no experience in retail at all. I was proven right after she made mistake after mistake and couldn't cope with the job.

I wasn't sorry when our general manager left; he didn't exactly make himself likeable. He even accused me of sucking up to him. All I did wrong was my job. It was obvious that my time there was ending. I couldn't work in a place where I wasn't respected or appreciated. I was the hardest worker, even when my health was bad.

Unfortunately, the new general manager wasn't any better. He let the kids run the place. The younger staff ran circles around him. When the next supervisor role came up, I went for it, and the new manager, who'd said go for it, turned me down. After five attempts and being screwed every time, I'd had enough!

I still had church. It was one night after praying that I had a moment of clarity. I felt like someone or something was telling me it was time to make peace — something that had bothered me for years — to write to an ex from Butlins. We ended badly, and I wanted to make it right. It was just after the second back operation that this came to me. While I was recovering, I sat and wrote one of the hardest yet most heartfelt letters I'd ever written. It took me several days to find the words. I still had her old address, as I'm sad enough to keep old letters. I posted it without looking back. That was that.

It was a Hail Mary. After three years without a woman, I didn't see that changing. The one saving grace was my friendships with my Butlins family. I still regularly called Louise, and one day she sent me a voice recording of her singing one of my favourite songs, *My Immortal* by Evanescence. I was blown away by her voice. I was the only person from Butlins that had ever heard her sing. That was a great honour. Then there was Phil. Even after our holiday to Kavos, we still tried to visit each other at least once a year. My mum enjoyed seeing him; he was like another son to her. The time together was precious, and I felt at peace when in his company. It was like that with all my Butlins friends. It's just a shame that I've not been able to see more of them.

February 2012, everything changed. It started with my back deteriorating. It was three months post-surgery when discomfort at the base of my spine got worse. The issues with my right leg came back, but not as bad as before. It was very hard to accept that even though the surgery had been a success, I had lasting problems. I was starting to wonder if I would ever be pain-free. I had already been on oral morphine for two years and other painkillers. I could tolerate the tablets to a degree, but the morphine had caused another issue. It was destroying my teeth. After four months of being on the Oramorph, my first tooth broke and had to be taken out. Then, three months later, a second broke. Every few months, another tooth or more would break and would need to come out — until I had a hair-raising moment. When the dentist tried to remove a tooth, she found it was brittle and came apart. Part went down the back of my throat and made me choke. I already had a bad gag reflex, so from then I would have to go to hospital to have any teeth out. Eventually, I'd need to be put under anaesthesia, as they took multiple out at a time until all were removed.

I knew Oramorph was an opiate and from the heroin family, but didn't understand back then the side effects. Anytime you meet a heroin addict, you'll likely see their teeth are all falling apart — and that is what happened to me. Out of all I'd been through since the fall on the ice, losing my teeth was the worst. Dentures are not fun, and it took seven years to lose all my teeth. My gums receded so much the dentures wouldn't stay in without Fixodent. Having to rely on that to eat normally was not fun. This would stop me going out to eat unless I had no choice. It also added to serious bouts of oral thrush. Oral thrush is unpleasant and leaves a bitter taste in your mouth. I even had to have an endoscopy to see how far it went. They found it all the way down my oesophagus to my stomach, which meant I have it for life. No amount of antibiotics or treatment will ever clear it fully.

February did have a flip side; I had a friend request on Facebook. The woman I sent the letter to didn't know the surname, so debated on how to respond. After a few days, I built up the courage to message asking who it was. A few days later, I got a reply—it was my ex. I couldn't believe it. Not only did she get the letter, but she actually wanted to talk to me. Time does heal some wounds.

We spent the next couple of weeks talking generally about what we had been up to. She told me her mum was still living in the same flat, so passed on the letter when it arrived. It didn't take long for us to both realise that we still had feelings for each other. We started to speak on the phone more frequently. It didn't feel like ten years since we last spoke. There was only one thing for it—we had to see each other. I was only working part time at this point, as my recovery was slow. This meant I could go away for a couple of nights.

I was excited at the thought of seeing her again. The journey down was hard on my health, but my excitement kept me going. Although, it caught up to me when I got back home. I remembered enough to find where she used to live. I found the road of her address and had to call to make sure I didn't end up somewhere I shouldn't. She was living in a high-rise and over halfway up. I was a little nervous, as my fears of being up high were in the back of my mind.

Then just like that, I was standing outside her door, full of hope and apprehension. It was surreal. It was one of those moments that you don't forget. There she was standing there, smiling at me. She was the same woman — although older — but to me, perfect in every way. She might have been my second love, but the deepest love I'd ever had.

We hugged and went inside; it felt like a dream. I didn't even try to hide the huge grin I had. I felt happy for the first time in far too long. Then she introduced me to her two daughters. Finally, I got a taste of what could have been — what being in a family was like.

It was one of the best days of my life. I was worn out from the travelling but buzzing to find out what I'd missed and excited to be close to this woman. The first kiss was magical, and had it not been for the kids, I would have dragged her into the bedroom. You can't blame me. When it was good, it was amazing — and I had gone three and a half years without a woman. I may have been less healthy than the last time we were together, but I was still a man with needs.

We had a nice family meal; she was the first woman to cook for me that was edible. The kids were a bit overexcited by bedtime, so it took them a while to fall asleep.

We had the flat to ourselves. The anticipation built to a crescendo. I knew she felt the same by the way we kissed. Bedtime didn't come soon enough, but it was worth the wait. It was a long night, but a lot of fun. I knew I'd found my happy place and couldn't ignore the love building inside of me. It was too early to say it out loud.

The next morning, I was smiling like the cat that had got the cream. I longed to be happy, and after many mistakes since Butlins, it felt like it had been worth it. That second day went by too quickly, but was enjoyable; the night wasn't bad either.

Just like that, it was time to say goodbye. I didn't think it would be so hard, but it was. I didn't want to leave, but knew I had to. The journey home was bittersweet, but I left on the promise that it was only the beginning.

Returning to work was a huge comedown after being on a high. It didn't help the rapid deterioration of my back; the pain got worse day by day. The only thing that kept me going was talking to my woman.

I only had to wait a few weeks before I was back down to Southampton, and it was even better. It was spring, and the weather was warmer. On Sunday, there was an event nearby, and we all went. We took a picnic and had the best day. It felt like all the pain and despair of the past few years were worth it. I was smitten and couldn't have loved her more. We both said those fateful words and meant them. I was only there for a couple of nights, and that wasn't long enough. We talked about next steps and the possibility of me moving in with her. There were some challenges ahead, and we both agreed it was what we wanted. Her kids seemed happy with me. It was harder leaving the second time, and I knew we couldn't stay apart for much longer. Her birthday was fast approaching; I planned to be romantic and cement our relationship before taking it further.

Work was torture, physically and emotionally. I really felt like an outsider and was getting tired of being treated like rubbish. It had been my longest job; I'd been there three and a half years, although had 16 months off sick. It started after the fall on the ice, when the pain was so bad that I couldn't cope. But after the first operation, I had a brief reprieve before the problems started up again. I was determined to fight it and not let the pain define me. I was proud of myself for fighting even when I wanted to give up.

There were days I wanted to crawl into a ball and hide. A constant battle that transcended anything I'd experienced previously.

The third time I went to Southampton, it was her birthday; I planned in my mind what I wanted to do. I'd bought a bottle of champagne, some candles, made a romantic playlist on my phone and cooked a nice meal. A perfect evening, at least, that was the plan until one of her friends popped round for a chat. The food was ready, but I had to wait until her friend left. Thankfully, my culinary skills were good enough, and the food held up. Before we sat down, she excused herself. She returned soon after, wearing the same top she wore the first night we met at Butlins. I remembered it well and had to smile. In many ways, it was the perfect evening; the food was great and the champagne was delicious. After dinner... let's just say it was a magical evening and memorable for all the right reasons.

The next day, we got serious and talked about me moving in. We both wanted it and knew it was inevitable. It was still hard leaving, but it was only for a short time, then we'd have the rest of our lives together. Least, that was the plan — but like any plan and dream, reality is usually very different.

I was happy handing my notice in. I'd given a month's notice out of respect for my time with the company. I'd be down to work a 26-hour week and end up only doing 12 hours. It was embarrassing and demoralising. It wasn't so much if, rather than when, I would have to give up work. I decided that it would be better to go while I still had some quality of life left. My final day was the 7th May 2012. I'd arranged a leaving do the previous Saturday and was disappointed that nobody came out. I knew I wasn't the most popular person, but I still thought I'd earned a farewell. That was the ultimate disrespect.

My final day wasn't any better. There was no fanfare, no good luck, no "hope you enjoy your new life". I did get a card in an envelope before I left. I'd spent a fair amount in the past for others, but got nothing on my exit. I've been brought up to not expect anything, but after giving so much, I thought somebody would care enough to do something for me. The final insult came when I opened the card and it was signed by less than half the staff, so I ripped it up and binned it. I was ashamed of them. It would end up being my last place of employment, and yet I was treated like I was nothing. I'd experienced some bad jobs in my time, but that job took the biscuit. I was glad I was going to be leaving the town, as I wouldn't want to see anyone I worked with, as it would be hard to hide my disdain.

Chapter 45

The day had come, and I was all packed again! It was the 9th May 2012, and I was moving in with another woman, but this time with someone who made me feel whole. It was perfect, I was truly happy. There was a lot of excitement about my arrival, but at a difficult time. Her grandad was in the hospital, and it was terminal. She found it hard balancing seeing him and looking after her kids, so I agreed to be there for them while she visited her grandad.

It started out fine with her visiting, and I was assured that if her girls played up and wouldn't listen, to message her and she would come back. Obviously, I was reluctant, as she wouldn't get another chance to see her relative. In the end, the kids wouldn't listen, and I was not in a position to discipline them. It was a difficult position to be in.

I enjoyed the family time we spent together, especially bedtime. The daily routine was the biggest challenge. I was so used to being up until 2:00 a.m. or 3:00 a.m., keeping an eye on my mum and making sure she got into bed. But going to bed by 10:00 p.m. was a shock, but not as bad as getting up at 6:30 a.m. I've never been a morning person.

We got to have a night out on my birthday; a table was booked at a restaurant in Southampton city centre. It was my first romantic night out with a partner. Although it was windy and a little chilly, the food was great and the company was better. I found myself looking into her eyes and feeling so lucky.

Then came the surprise! At the end of May, on a Saturday morning, three weeks after moving in, my girlfriend told me she was pregnant. Talk about a bombshell. At first, I was in shock, then a huge grin spread across my face. Goody, you still got it! Then I asked her how sure she was. She said she had taken one test and asked me to pick up a couple more to be sure. I had to hold my excitement so that the kids wouldn't hear me and start asking questions.

Once I got back, the anticipation was building until she came out of the toilet and started smiling. I felt like the luckiest man alive. We had talked about having a baby together, but didn't think it would happen so quickly. She fell pregnant within days of me moving in – that's three and a half years of celibacy for you. I started thinking about when I was married, and apart from the miscarriage, nothing happened. Either someone was looking down on me, or it was just blind luck that it happened with someone I truly loved. Looking at my partner, knowing she had my baby inside of her, I felt so much love. The world could have ended, and I still would have been smiling.

We then told her daughters, and the eldest was excited. She was eight, and the youngest was four – the younger one didn't understand. I couldn't wait to call my mum and tell her the good news; she was so happy for me, and shocked. I wanted to stand on the rooftops and shout it out, but then I remembered I didn't do heights.

When we got together, I had a dream of how I wanted things to go. I was that confident we were perfect together. I had a tattoo done before moving down – of red roses on my chest, as they were her favourite flower – and the first letter of her name. I'd decided that if we got engaged, then married and had a baby, I'd get the rest of her name tattooed. Always the dreamer, me!

The buzz from finding out she was pregnant took a while to wear off. I never thought anything else would happen between us, but I guess fate had other ideas. Home life was good – until her grandad passed away. It was tough, but she was taking it reasonably well – at least I thought she was. I was starting to learn an awful lot about my partner.

I did what I could to comfort her, but she brushed me off. I'd try until she said she wanted to be left alone. I'm a bit of a touchy-touchy, feely-feely kind of person. I like to hug and feel the comfort of another, especially through tough times, but not her. It was very different to what I was used to. That was how it went that first week, and then those cracks crept up on me so fast I was spinning.

It started when I woke up one morning – my snoring had kept her up on two consecutive nights, and she had to sleep on the sofa. I told her I was sorry and that it was a side effect from the nasal surgery I had in 2005. This was the first time a partner had told me it was a problem. Even though I was made to buy a multitude of anti-snoring products, I said I would sleep on the sofa. What I didn't foresee was that I'd stay there.

That ended any closeness between us. Of course, I'd never dream of doing anything that wasn't wanted, but I did miss the connection. I tried to be a caring and loving partner, bending over backwards for her and her kids. Even her kids started resenting me. Their mum was drinking more and would disappear for most of the day.

The longer it went on, the further apart we got. The only time we really talked was when arguing over the most benign things. The worst one was the day of the first baby scan. It should have been the happiest day of my life, seeing my baby for the first time. Inside, I was torn; part of me was over the moon seeing this tiny life growing inside the woman I still loved. On the outside, I was falling apart and couldn't remember the last time I smiled. I knew it wasn't a healthy place to be when she was still so early in her pregnancy.

When we got back to the flat, the arguing started up again. Most of the time, it was over stupid things. It wasn't helped by my sleeping on a 2-seater sofa. My back was getting worse. I was lucky to get five hours' sleep a night.

That's when I noticed the weight loss. Every day, I was non-stop. I had no problem with shopping and housework; I thought she would have wanted to be more involved as a family. I still held out hope that things would improve and we would enjoy the new life we had created. Perhaps I was so naïve to what a woman goes through during pregnancy and dealing with a loss at the same time. But I figured that in a relationship, you would lean on your partner for support. I was being pushed further and further away until I felt like an outsider.

I'd been living there for nine weeks and sleeping on the sofa for three when the pain became unbearable. I went to the local doctor's for help. The man I saw was nice, and after speaking for ten minutes, I think he realised that something was wrong. He said that he wanted to see me every week. I didn't read too much into it at the time; I didn't understand how intuitive he was until the following week.

It had been a particularly bad day with constant arguing; I had just had enough and left the flat in tears. I started wandering until I realised how close I was to the railway line – more specifically, the bridge that went over it. It wasn't especially warm, so not many people were around. I went to the centre of the bridge and looked over it. The emotions took over, and I felt like I'd reached a point of no return. I realised how easy it would be to climb up and wait for the next train. Then just fall forward and it would be all over – the pain, the heartache – done, finished. I didn't even care that I was going to be a dad. I've been in some very low places in my life, but none were as bad as that day. I should have been full of joy at being a father, but I just wanted it to end! I truly believed my partner wouldn't shed a tear. The only people who would miss me were my mum, my sister and a few friends from Butlins, but they'd get over it. I'd made up my mind I was going to end it all.

Then my mobile rang. It was as though the spell was broken. It brought me back to reality. Of course, it was my partner wanting to know where I was, which was followed by another argument. I was so wound up, I left the bridge and walked back to the flat. I didn't tell anyone what I almost did.

The next time I went to the doctor's, I let slip how bad things had gotten, and he put me on antidepressants. I'm sure if I told him what I almost did, he would have had me sectioned and on suicide watch. My face must have given away my true feelings. I couldn't remember the last time I'd eaten a proper meal or had a good night's sleep. I was a zombie. Unless you have gotten close to ending it, it's hard to explain what it feels like. I wasn't proud of myself for letting it get so bad that I couldn't see any way out.

It got worse, believe it or not. Not only was I getting daily abuse from my partner, as I couldn't do anything right, her kids joined in – hitting me and spitting at me – then my partner's mum got involved. It became a daily barrage from every direction, and there wasn't a thing I could do about it. I was in the kitchen one afternoon when she came in and said, 'Don't you dare treat your kid any different to the girls,' and on it went with her pointing her finger at my face.

I had been so beaten down, I just said, 'I won't,' hoping she would leave me alone. I wanted to yell back and tell her they are not my children and never would be. I wasn't a father to them, nor would I try to be. They had their own absent fathers. It wasn't my fault, and although I treated them right, respect had to be earned, and neither had earned it from me. I still fed them, changed the beds, did the ironing and the shopping even when I was struggling to stay on my feet. I don't think any of them understood the seriousness of my health issues or the pain I was in daily. I never complained.

I was pushed further over the edge and once again found myself heading towards that railway bridge. This time, I had no tears, no feelings, just acceptance that my fate was sealed. I wasn't wanted, I wasn't respected, and I certainly wasn't loved, so what was the point in fighting a lost cause? This time, I knew I could do it. Nobody knew where I was or what I was planning. I knew I wasn't perfect! I tried to be a good partner and backed off when she wanted to be alone. Nothing seemed to be enough. I was ready to take those last few steps and get it over with.

But once again, my phone rang. Another argument followed. Enough was enough. I walked back to the flat feeling dejected that I couldn't be left alone for half an hour, yet when I was indoors, I was nothing more than a hindrance.

A couple of days later, I bit the bullet. I regularly called my mum, and she'd known something was wrong for a while – after all, she knew me better than anyone. I walked out of the flat and broke down, telling her what was happening and how bad things were.

She was heartbroken, and I could tell she was crying too. She told me not to worry, she would help me. For the first time in weeks, there was hope; there was a possibility that the nightmare would end without me taking my own life.

Then, an hour later, I got a call from my sister. She told me she'd had a word with the man who had brought me down twelve weeks prior. He could pick me up three days later. I told her I had no money and couldn't afford it. She told me not to worry — it would be sorted. I could pay her back once I got straight. I was so relieved I broke down again. I didn't feel any guilt for leaving the woman I still loved. I wasn't stupid enough to think there was hope of reconciliation. I knew if I went back to that bridge a third time, I would have jumped. I doubted I'd be saved a third time.

I knew I couldn't tell her I was leaving, as two days later was her grandad's funeral. I would be leaving the day afterwards. If I wanted to be a dad, I had to leave, no matter how hard it was. Those were the very longest two days of my life.

The day before the funeral, she had her cousin stay over. It was the first time in six weeks that I would get to sleep in her bed. I was in the bedroom while she sat and drank a bottle of vodka with her 16-year-old cousin. Sometimes I wondered if she even wanted to have our baby. She didn't act like it!

I wanted to take the alcohol off her, but feared she would get physical. She was aggressive when drinking, and we ended up having another argument that night. I finally had the guts to stand up for myself. I'm not proud of what I said. I told her, "In the last few weeks I've felt like I'm nothing more than a lodger and a babysitter," to which she replied, "If that's the way you feel, after tomorrow (the funeral), I won't have to worry, as I won't have to look after her girls ever again," which was followed by her telling me that after the funeral, she would have one drink and then come back. Like a fool, I believed her.

I didn't sleep that night and spent most of the night watching the door, expecting someone to come in and beat me up. Somehow that didn't happen, and I just had one more day and night to get through. The next morning, little was said between us. I was left to look after her two daughters and a cousin who was too young to go to the funeral. While they were kept busy with the TV and some colouring books, I closed the bedroom door and tried to pack. It wasn't easy, and I didn't have enough boxes. I couldn't leave the kids on their own for long, and I certainly couldn't trust them.

The funeral was at lunchtime, and although I was busy packing and every now and then checking on the kids, I was constantly on edge, by 3:00 p.m. I texted to see when she was coming back. I wasn't surprised when she didn't reply. As time flew by, I realised that she wouldn't be coming back when she said she would. I knew it was a tough day, so I tried to remain sympathetic; it wasn't easy.

By 5:00 p.m., her cousin turned up to pick his sister up, and he told me my girlfriend would be along soon. I knew I was on her time, and she'd arrive when she wanted. It was after 8:00 p.m. when she got back. I'd already given up trying to do anything with her daughters. As soon as she came into her bedroom and saw all the boxes and my belongings packed, she lost it. She had been drinking heavily again. I asked her what she expected when she hadn't shown me any sign she wanted me there. It was another dreadful night on edge, not sleeping, stuck in the bedroom waiting for something bad to happen. I really felt as though I was a prisoner. It was a bad place to be, torn between wanting to run into my girlfriend's arms and tell her I was sorry and beg for forgiveness, and the other side just wanted to get away as soon as possible. I counted down the hours.

By the morning, I was a nervous wreck. It was made worse when I tried to run a bath and my partner kept turning the heating off, so it was freezing cold. Then she said she was taking her girls so they didn't have to see me go, and then they left, leaving her cousin there to make sure I went quietly. I managed to get a semi-warm bath and be done in record time.

While all this was going on, I was in contact with my mate from town who had come along to give me moral support. I was so relieved when I got the text that they were just parking up. As soon as I saw my friend, I knew the nightmare was nearly over. It didn't take long for the three of us to load up the van. I dropped the keys off at the flat and left. I hated myself for being weak, for letting myself be beaten down until there was nothing left, for walking away from potentially my one true love, and for not being able to fight for that love. I'd failed so spectacularly that I had nothing left inside, and I was about to shut down completely.

You hear so often about women suffering terrible relationships and being treated as though they are worthless, and that it's always the men who are the aggressors. What they don't tell you is that it can be just as bad in reverse. Men do have feelings. Men can be pushed to the limit and made to feel worthless. Suicide in men is much higher than women. It's not talked about enough. I was lucky I managed to open up before I did do something final. It is sad when all you want to do is love and be loved and not have it in return. It can go downhill very quickly. If this ever happens to you, or you think someone is going through something similar — whether male or female — reach out, show them a helping hand, and make sure they know there is another way. There is a way out that doesn't end with them in a hole in the ground. Don't be afraid to stand up and help. You really could save a life!

Chapter 46

We'd been driving for just over an hour when my mobile rang. It was her. I panicked. I couldn't answer, I couldn't face whatever was coming, so I declined the call. I then panicked. I called my service provider and begged for a new number. They agreed and didn't charge me. I felt bad for doing it, but I couldn't face any more drama. Her voice would've made me crumble. She had a power over me like no other woman.

My mate did his best to keep me upbeat, but it was difficult when I was so conflicted. I still wished I was back in Southampton. I knew it wouldn't work, no matter how much I wanted it to. Time would tell if there was a way back. We had a baby on the way, so I would see her again. If our relationship was unsalvageable, then being parents would have to be enough.

Once we got to the other side of London, I felt able to breathe again. I was still tense and was dreading facing my parents, as I felt like a failure. The shame of leaving a pregnant woman would haunt me for a long time. I believed it was for the right reasons. At the back of my mind, I kept telling myself I was a coward.

I was relieved to see my mum. Although I'd only been gone 12 weeks, it felt much longer. My mum instantly noticed how much weight I'd lost. It wasn't until I weighed myself and saw it was over a stone and a half. When depression, anxiety and always being on the go take their toll. I knew I hadn't eaten enough; it would take a long time to get back to normal.

That night I slept 12 hours. Like eating, it had been a long time since I'd had enough! It was so quiet compared to what I'd gotten used to. No kids waking me up at 6:30 in the morning, no rushing out to go shopping. All of a sudden, I had nothing to do, nowhere to be, and nobody to care for. It was surreal and depressing.

A couple of days after moving back, I texted my ex and said it was my new number. I didn't know what else to say. I couldn't say I missed her or ask her how they were. I got no reply, but that would change. The biggest shock at home was my inability to show emotion. I couldn't smile, laugh, cry — nothing! It was as though my emotions had been switched off. I had a constant blank face, almost as if the lights were on but nobody was home. I think that frightened my mum more than anything else. Nobody knew what to say or do, so just left me alone.

One morning, my mum told me that she was so scared the night before. I'd been so quiet in my room she sent my dad to check on me. He had to lean over me to check I was breathing. I'd told them about the snoring, and they couldn't believe it. Made me wonder what could cause me to snore while in Southampton but not at my parents'. I wondered if my ex just wanted me out of the bedroom. I was starting to see things that weren't there. I really didn't know what to think anymore—I was a mess.

Slowly but surely, I started to crawl out of the slumber. It took me a whole month before the mask slipped away and I was able to smile again. I found little to smile about but did my best for my mum's sake. Nobody likes to upset their mother, especially when they are your greatest advocate.

Just before the second baby scan was due, I decided I had to do something. I remembered from the first scan how much the pictures cost. I put £10 in a stamped addressed envelope with a letter. I told her I'd put the money in to cover four copies. I asked her to use the money and please send me a photo. That was also when she would find out if it was a boy or a girl. I would have loved a boy, but as long as the baby was healthy, I'd be happy.

The day after the scan, I received the envelope back with the money and no photo. I was gutted; it was cruel. I'd never asked her for anything and felt like she was punishing me. It set off my anxiety and depression—I was beginning to crack. I backed off and waited for her to contact me. I longed to hear her voice, to know she was okay and that our baby was fine. I wanted to be able to talk to our child through her belly and feel the first kick. All the dreams I had, that I came so close to achieving, had been ripped from my grasp and I had nobody to blame but myself. I hated myself and spent many nights kicking myself. I'd dream about what could have been. Then I'd wake and be devastated all over again.

I did send a text message to her, hoping that there was a way to start rebuilding the bridges. I got an eventual reply saying she wanted to be left alone and she would contact me when she was ready. I had no choice. She had me wrapped around her little finger and she knew it. Maybe I was gullible or just that desperate to please, or maybe I just loved her so much I was blinded.

It wasn't just my emotions and my mental health that took a downward slide. My physical health deteriorated too. After being on the go without a break, then suddenly doing very little, had a negative effect. All that time I was struggling prior to moving to Southampton hit me all at once! I had to start using a crutch to support my walking. My balance was terrible and, without the crutch, I was prone to my legs giving way on me. It got scary, and I had a genuine fear of the stairs. Yes, the stairs. I struggled to lift my feet, which would lead to me falling up and down stairs. Being a father started to scare me. Just the thought of being unable to hold my child safely frightened me!

Although I wasn't with my child's mother, I still felt that I had a duty. Christmas 2012, I went out of my way to buy presents for my ex and her kids. I wanted to show that even though I left, I still wanted to be a family. I didn't write a letter and never asked for anything, but hoped it would be enough for her to say thank you. I was fooling myself.

I kept my mobile phone close just in case she would contact me. Say she wanted to make peace for our child. She did message two weeks before the due date asking for money, which I did. I would do anything for them both.

Our baby was due on Friday 1st February 2013. I waited and waited, but no news. I thought either she hadn't given birth or she was punishing me again—it was torture not knowing! By the Wednesday, I couldn't take it any more. I messaged her early and asked if there was any news. I was polite. No reply. Then that afternoon I received a very angry phone call. I was shocked how nasty she was to me. She said she was fed up with everyone asking what was happening. My reply was simply, 'I am the father and needed to know,' which was followed by her very impolite, 'Are you?' That hurt, and was low even for her. There was more arguing. I couldn't take it any more, so hung up before saying something I'd regret.

I woke up the Sunday morning anxious, stuck between a rock and a hard place.

I'd considered going to Southampton and sleeping on a bench. I knew she wouldn't have let me in the room with her, but I'd be at the hospital. In the end, I held back and waited.

Then, late Sunday morning, I got the text message I'd been hoping for. My son was born healthy the night before at 11:52 p.m. The date was 9th February 2013. She was obviously tired, hence telling me the next day, but at least she told me.

I went flying down the stairs to tell my mum, with a huge grin on my face, even if it was bittersweet. My dream of being a father had finally come true, although I had to wait until I was 33. I called my best friend and told him, and we agreed to meet and go down the pub to celebrate. It was early afternoon, and we had not long been drinking our first pint when my phone buzzed. It was a picture of my son — my beautiful, perfect little son. I couldn't stop smiling; I almost cried. I wasn't the first face our boy saw — that broke my heart.

My heart was full of pride while my mind tossed and turned like an insomniac. I smiled at my friend and tried to enjoy the moment of becoming a father. What I didn't know was that I'd had it easy compared to what I was about to experience.

I couldn't wait to get home and show my mum the photo of her first and only grandson. I knew she would be happy, as she wanted many grandchildren—almost as much as I had longed to be a father. When I showed my dad, he just shrugged and couldn't care less. I would receive a second photo a few days later and would be equally overjoyed. I hoped that now our child was born, my ex would be more open to us being parents. There was always doubt in my mind that it was too good to be true. I decided I'd take action to protect myself, just in case.

A week after my son was born, she told me his name. I was in shock; we had talked about names early on, before everything went downhill. I thought we had an agreement, but once again I was wrong. She told me she'd asked her girls what they wanted to call their brother, and what they chose stuck. I should have known. There wasn't a thing I could do about it. The final straw was when I called her and asked when she was registering the birth so I could be there. She said she'd already done it. I was devastated—everything sacred when your child is born taken from me. I asked why she didn't tell me, and she said it had nothing to do with me. I knew then she wouldn't be fair; she wasn't going to include me. It was time I took back some control. It was time I stood up and be a man. It was time to take action.

I visited a local solicitor — it was the same one that handled my divorce. I suppose it would be fitting the same one would help me to gain my rights as a father. I told the lady everything that I could about how I ended up leaving my ex and what had happened after my son was born. It was just before legal aid was finished, so I knew I'd get financial help. I hadn't worked since leaving the cinema and it looked like I never would work again. My health had gotten worse, with no way back. The lady was very understanding and asked what I wanted, and then she went through the process. I would have to go to court to claim my parental responsibilities and get a visitation order so I was allowed access to my son. She told me that the only way I would be denied was if it was proven I had violent tendencies or if I had a drug or alcohol problem — basically anything that would be a negative towards my boy. I'd never raised a hand to a woman, I barely drank and wouldn't touch drugs — I had enough with the prescribed ones for the pain. I felt safe I'd have no problems. I told her I was allowed to visit my son soon and could we review afterwards. She said yes, and we left it at that.

Chapter 47

It was 4 weeks after his birth that I met my son for the first time. I was excited and nervous at the prospect of holding my son. I was gutted I had to wait so long, but it was on his mum's time, not mine, and I couldn't afford to alienate her. I decided I was going to go down looking my best. I hoped that this would be the start of mending what was broken. I still held hope that our relationship wasn't completely over. Although I am a realist, I still had optimism.

I'd booked a B&B for one night so I could go down the day before I was due to see my son. I knew the travelling would take it out of me. I went by bus, as it was cheaper, and had spent money on clothes, nappies and other things that I thought she would need. I'd even bought a teddy so he would have something from me to keep. I'd packed my best suit and tie with a white shirt. I was ready — or at least, I thought I was.

The journey was horrible. It felt like my body was being ripped apart over and over again — and that was just to London. I had an hour before the next bus and wasn't looking forward to it. To give you an idea what it's like to have back pain: every bump is like a hammer, hit into your spine — but on a motorway that has many bumps, it's a constant stream of pain. It feels like it will never end. The only thing that kept me going was knowing I'd be holding my son soon. The love of your child is a very strong motivator.

The B&B was nothing special, but it was for only one night, so I wasn't too worried. I didn't sleep well either — partly excitement, but mostly apprehension. I didn't know the reception I would get when I arrived. Regardless of everything I'd been through, I still loved my ex and still wanted to spend the rest of my life with her.

I was suited and booted and shaking with anticipation — a great way to start the day. I was told that I could only visit when her girls were at school, on weekdays and between 9:30 a.m.– 2:30 p.m. I arrived at her flat just after 11:30 a.m. After a few deep breaths and the hope I didn't crumble, I knocked and prayed.

The door was opened by my ex's mum. I must have had shock on my face, as she quickly explained that she was asked to be there as support. I didn't know what they thought I was going to say or do. I wanted to see my son but also his mum. I knew that I'd go weak at the knees and would want to take her in my arms. In reality, it was baby steps — no pun intended. Some people can affect you in a way so profound that it doesn't matter if it's been a month, a year, or a decade: that attraction has your pulse racing and your face flushed, because some feelings cannot be denied.

She let me in, and I walked down the long hallway. I came to the living room door, as out came my ex holding our baby son. I just froze as I took in every little detail.

His tiny hands, his tiny feet, the small amount of hair, even the little gurgling he was making. He was perfect in every single way. She actually smiled, and that gave me the smallest ray of hope. We went into her living room, and then she handed me our baby boy. I knew the correct way to hold a baby and took him willingly. I was finally complete; I was tempted to hold him high like the *Lion King* moment. Instead, I just held him close to my chest and cherished the moment. I had my camera on me and asked to have some photos taken for me. That day, like every day after that I saw him, would be held deep in my memories. It truly was a special moment for me.

After being there half an hour, I'd handed over everything I had bought, and the chatting became easier. I got to hold my son a few times, and my ex said his nappy needed changing. She laid our son on the floor, and I joined her. We were so close we were touching, and instantly there were sparks. I knew she felt it too by the way she almost shivered. It felt so natural to be that close to the two people I loved the most. Little was said. Once the nappy was changed, we stood, and the electricity between us faded.

Conversation became easier, and her mum watched us at a safe distance. I would later be told that her mum could see there was still something there between us. After I'd been there an hour and a half, it was time to leave. I'd assured her that I wouldn't overstay my welcome and knew it was small steps. It was so hard going; I wanted to be there for my son's bedtime and kiss him goodnight. It would make it feel more real to me. I didn't mention the birth certificate that day, as I didn't want to rock the boat. It was hard biting my tongue when so much needed to be said.

We walked to the door; our son was asleep by then. I was so desperate to lean forward and kiss her — I couldn't risk it. I left with photos and videos that were a little jumpy due to my nervousness and anxiety. No nastiness, no bad words, no refusal to more visits. I had hope — it had been a very long time since I felt any, but that day I did.

I knew the journey home was going to be painful. I managed to shut out a lot of the pain, not enough to escape completely. I spent most of the journey looking at the photos and going over what was said. Not an easy task, but decided that overall, it went well. I held my son, and there was hope for the future. What that future looks like, only time will tell. Once I was back home, I was so happy to show my mum the pictures; she smiled with me. It helped that he was so adorable. My mind kept drifting to that moment when we were on the floor, when we touched, whether by accident or by design. We had looked at each other at the same time, and the fire between us was clearly still there. I hoped that the next time I was down, we would go one step further. It was around this time I decided I couldn't spend the rest of my life hoping I will be able to work again! I decided to volunteer at a local charity shop. The plan was to build myself back up and get fit enough to start a paid job. I had good intentions but wouldn't achieve that goal. To make matters worse, I pulled a muscle in my left shoulder that was so bad I ended up having to use a second crutch. It was frustrating; the harder I tried to get my life back, the worse I got. After that first visit, I felt that there had been good progress with my ex. I returned to the solicitors. I told them that things went well. I said I didn't want to rock the boat and believed my ex would be reasonable. The solicitor agreed that doing it out of the courts was always the better option and wished me luck. Another big mistake. I tried to see the best in people; sometimes I was just blind. This would be by far the worst mistake I made. I literally gave up any control I had or could have had by trusting the woman I loved.

It was six weeks later I got to see my son again. I was just as excited. I booked a B&B for two nights so I would get two days to spend with my son and his mum. I'd kept up a good dialogue since the first visit. I even went out and bought a bottle of champagne so that we could finally celebrate, plus it was just after her birthday and I wanted to do something special. I was always a hopeless romantic.

I took the bus down again, and the second time was even worse than the first. I didn't think it could have been that bad. I may not have been there 24/7, but I was going to do what I could for my son, by buying what I could for him. I didn't do it to impress his mum, but she did seem happy with the effort. Small steps. It wasn't long after I got to hers and given her what I'd bought when we kissed. It was a very chaste kiss, but it was progress. My heart was beating so fast I thought it was going to jump out of my chest. I was happy. I knew it was only a kiss, but it meant a lot to me.

It was difficult holding my son and trying to take photos and videos — not just for me to relive when I wasn't with him, but also so I could show my mum and friends. After all, he was a gorgeous baby. He may not have had much hair, but he had the brightest blue eyes I'd ever seen. They were like a blue sky on a summer's day. I knew that one day, his eyes alone would make girls swoon over him. He was going to be a daddy's boy — at least, I hoped so. I just needed to keep his mum sweet and stay in her good graces. It was on the second day I tentatively asked about being put on the birth certificate. I knew I had to tread carefully, as she could flip like a switch. Her response was simply, 'I will see how it goes.' I was frustrated, but she had all the power. It wasn't all sunshine and flowers. Prior to my second visit, she called to tell me she had taken our son to have professional photos done. I wasn't happy, as I thought that was the sort of thing you would discuss first. Don't get me wrong — any photos of my son is a good thing — but being expected to find money for a copy out of the blue wasn't easy. Of course, I paid and got a photo that has been on my bedroom wall ever since. I've always believed that parenting should be done together, with mutual consent, so both parties get a fair shake. There is nothing worse than feeling like you have no control and being forced into something. Still being so young, I figured it would have been better when he was older and able to sit up at least. But what did I know? I'd never had a child before.

I was understanding many things. My friend Louise once said to me, 'You never know true love until you hold your child for the first time.' The first time I saw my son, I understood. The second visit, my love grew stronger. He was the centre of my universe and nothing else mattered. Leaving was hard, and as I was going down in the lift, I wanted to turn around and go back and never leave. I couldn't, but I could dream. At least we had gotten closer; I didn't know if she felt the same way, even though we'd said the words.

Then everything changed; my life was turned upside down. It was May 2013, my mum was taken ill and rushed to hospital. She had gotten sepsis in her leg due to the diabetes. We didn't know how bad it was at first. I had been in to visit her two days before she took a downward slide. On the Thursday, for some reason, I had an upset stomach, so didn't go in to visit her. She was told that she would have to have her leg amputated below the knee to save her life! The doctors had told her a couple of months earlier it would need doing. But she was determined to keep her leg. With her lack of mobility and already needing a wheelchair, she was scared. But that Thursday evening, my dad got a phone call, saying to come in and convince my mum to have the operation, otherwise she had days to live.

We rushed to the hospital that evening. I couldn't lose my mum; she was the glue that kept our family together. On the way there, we passed an ambulance that had tipped over at a roundabout — it felt like a bad omen.

My mum was on oxygen and looked so ill, I was scared. She knew why we were there and cried so hard it broke my heart. I'd seen my mum cry many times, but not like that. I begged her, told her we needed her and couldn't lose her. Eventually, she agreed to do it and signed the paperwork. She was booked to have the surgery the next day. We had to leave; I hoped that she would be better by the next evening. No such luck.

That night, she took a turn for the worse and was rushed into ICU, losing consciousness. The next day, we were told what had happened. We visited, and seeing my mum hooked up to multiple tubes and breathing apparatus was dreadful. I admit I cried and prayed she would pull through. I sat and held her hand and talked to her, telling her how much we all loved her and needed her.

The next day was Saturday. The family was asked to speak with the consultant to discuss next steps. Even my brother attended and tried to take over — being a doctor in chemistry, he thought he knew it all. Some people have to be the centre of attention. My mum's sister was present, but only because she was afraid she'd miss something. The consultant told us that the sepsis had progressed. If she woke up soon, they could perform the amputation. He said to be prepared that she may never wake up. The following four days were spent holding her hand and begging her to wake up. I even told my friend he better get up there quick to see her. Ironically, when he went in, my mum started to show signs of life. We were hugely relieved but knew she was far from out of the woods.

By the Friday, my mum was well enough to have the surgery. We waited at home for news, but her sister decided not to tell us the surgery got delayed — we'd been panicking. Until that evening, when we were told the surgery was successful and she was doing well.

The next day was my birthday, and I had the best present I could have asked for. I got to the hospital where my mum was sitting up, as though she hadn't been at death's door. There were tears, but this time of joy and relief. We would find out months later that she had a heart attack while unconscious. She was very lucky. She'd end up spending over two months in hospital. She needed physio to get used to the amputation. She was safe, which was the main thing. It was a year of ups and downs; I was grateful for the ups. More were coming.

Chapter 48

July 2013, I was back in Southampton for another visit. This time, though, I would take the train. It was more expensive but saved my health. The tubes in London were a nightmare on crutches; it was so hot down there I was sweating by the time I got the train I needed. The things we do for an easier life.

Like the last two times I visited, the first day was spent settling into the B&B. I didn't have much of an appetite but knew I had to eat something. Although I was worn out and excited at holding my son again, sleep was hard to come by. What I didn't know was it would be the only sleep I'd get in the two nights I was there.

When I arrived at the flat, it was all smiles. We embraced and then went to our son. I was amazed how fast he was growing – except his hair. He was the most beautiful creature I'd ever seen; I'm sure every parent says that. I loved being a father! Although I wasn't there every day, I enjoyed the time I got. I got to spend over five hours there that day. It was difficult trying to spend time with my son whilst taking photos and videos.

I asked his mum to take some; she wasn't too keen. I did it by holding my son with one hand and my mobile with the other.

Fortunately, I was either on the floor with my son or sitting on the sofa. His safety was always my priority.

It was hard with my son being unsure of me; the few days I'd gotten with him weren't enough to make him feel comfortable with me. I tried my best to make it fun for him; I did get the odd smile out of him. But every second we were together, good or bad, was a gift. It didn't hurt that his mum and I were getting closer. The fire was lit, and it was just a matter of time before things went further. I managed to stay until she had to pick her daughters up from school.

Getting the bus back to the B&B was uneventful. We had talked about me going back later that evening when the kids were in bed. I spent the afternoon at the B&B. We were messaging each other when she had some bad news. I asked if she had eaten, and she said no, so I made arrangements to go to McDonald's and take it round by 8:00 p.m.

I'd gotten the food and had to wait longer than planned for the next bus – yeah, I didn't plan it very well. When I got to her flat, her eldest daughter was still up and had said she wanted to see me, which was a surprise. I'd been led to believe she hated me and never wanted to see me again. The food was cold by the time we got round to eating it, but neither of us were that bothered.

I finally got to say goodnight to my son for the first time. I finally felt like a proper dad! It was a special moment for me. I just stared at him as he slept, soaking it in and watching his chest rise and fall with every breath. Perfect!

After her daughter went to bed, we spent time in the kitchen chatting; the anticipation was building. I knew I wasn't leaving that night! When the time came for bed, it was worth the wait. It was like when I moved in – my world felt complete. It would be the one and only time I ever made love to a woman, and I'm not ashamed to admit it. The only downside was my health problems became an issue, with my shoulders and knees hurting. It wasn't quite the dream night I had hoped for. But she wasn't disappointed. I wasn't able to get any sleep, although my pains had eased. It was being told I had to leave before her girls woke up at 5:30 a.m. that spoilt it. I found myself sneaking out like a teenager. It was almost amusing, but at the same time I felt degraded. I had shown her how much I loved her and my willingness to drop everything when she needed me. I still hoped that we would become a family one day.

Waiting for the bus back to the B&B, I had plenty of time to work through what happened and what it meant. Eventually, I knew I just had to wait and see – I was still on her time.

First thing I did when I got back was take a long, warm shower to wake myself up.

There was no chance I could sleep, partly because I was still wired but also as I didn't want to miss time with my son. I knew it would be at least two months before I could go back due to the summer holidays, so had to make the most of the time I had. One thing I did learn was that even at four and a half months old, my son slept through the night.

Apparently, he did most nights. He was his father's boy, that's for sure. I may have had trouble getting to sleep, but once I'm out, I'm out for the duration.

When I went back, it was all smiles. As she was in a good mood, I decided to make the most of it. I asked about going on the birth certificate; her response was 'let's see how it goes', which was her way of stringing me along. It was very important to me; I knew I was a father, I'd seen and held my son, but there wasn't any legal document saying I was a father. It might seem trivial to some, but to me it meant everything. Plus, heaven forbid something happened to his mum, at least then he knew who his father was. Although I still wanted a relationship, she didn't feel the same. I felt used!

Then I made a fatal mistake. I told her I looked forward to the day when I can take my son to meet my parents. Like a switch flipping, she went ballistic at me, asking how I expected that to happen. I was shocked. It boiled down to her saying that she didn't want to see my parents, and her girls wouldn't either. I asked her if she meant that our son would never leave her side for the rest of his life, and she said yes. Telling her she was being unreasonable didn't go down well. All the good from the night before went down the toilet and made the next couple of hours uncomfortable. I ended up leaving earlier than planned. I was heart-broken. I don't think she cared that our son had a whole family he hadn't met. I thought that she'd be happy for our child to know both sides of his family.

I left feeling deflated. On one side, it was an almost perfect night together, followed by a day of disaster. My head was spinning, and the journey home was the worst way to burn off the excess energy coursing through my veins. It gave me time to get my head on straight for when I got home. I thought that would be the worst that I'd go through, but the next few months would be torture. I'd only poked the bear; I was about to wake it up from hibernation when it was at its hungriest.

The summer holidays had started and all seemed to be okay, so much so she actually sent me a photo of our son – the first since he was born. I was so happy; I wasn't hard to please. It was a beautiful photo of him smiling – it was priceless. I didn't get many smiles out of him when I visited. That was the last enjoyment I would get for a while – and the last photo.

She did something very rare and put the same photo up on Facebook, which I thought was a nice touch. The problem came when her cousin commented, saying he was gorgeous, just like his Godfather. I remarked, saying that he couldn't be unless he was christened, in which he replied he will be soon enough. I was christened and always planned to have any children I had christened too. Due to the fragile nature of my relationship with my ex, I never brought it up. But it was the sort of thing I would have thought we would discuss together. I did the only thing I thought was right and asked her if she was planning to christen our son. She said she was thinking about it. I challenged her by saying that I hoped she would tell me first so I could be there, in which she said no. She didn't want me there, and her girls didn't want to see me. I thought that her eldest at least didn't hate me. I tried to bargain and say I'd be at the back, out of the way, as long as I'm there.

She wasn't interested, and considering I was the one who went to church and I believed it was a rite of passage, I knew that no matter what I said, I wouldn't get through to her. In the end, her answer was to block me on Facebook. I could still communicate through text messaging or phone calls, but calling was not an option. Then she used her power and stopped me from seeing my son.

It would take weeks of begging before I was allowed to see him again. It was 16 weeks between visits; it was October when I finally got to go back. I was dreading it in case my ex decided to make life harder or just be negative, which was the last thing I wanted around my son. I wanted it to be a good, positive environment filled with love and happiness. But we rarely get what we want.

It started out strained, with no romance. I was only there for one day due to how uncomfortable our communications had been. By the end of the visit, we were more relaxed. There was still more work to do, but overall, it wasn't the worst visit.

I did get some great photos of my son and me together; he had a fascination with my crucifix necklace – probably because he was teething. I was sitting on the floor with my back to the sofa and had my son on my chest.

The next visit was in December. She told me it would have to be early December – so an early Christmas. I was excited; it was my first Christmas as a dad. I'd gone a bit mad on presents;

it wasn't hard buying for a 10-month-old baby. I never asked what she wanted for him, as I didn't want to be influenced. I also wanted to prove my worth as a father in getting decent presents. I knew he couldn't speak, but did hope that somehow he would like what I got. I also made sure his mum didn't go without. Like Birthday and Mother's Day, it was my duty as the father to get the mummy cards and buy mummy presents.

The icing on the cake was when I got to hear 'da da'. My smile beamed from one side of my face to the other. Nothing was more special than hearing those words. I didn't know it would be the first and last time I'd hear it. Thankfully, I got it on video. That first time was special in many ways, and years later, I can still remember it like it was yesterday. I've often been told I have a great memory, but when you have as much time on your hands as I do, your memories are sometimes all you have to keep you going.

That first day was no different from the first one back in July – all went well, plenty of smiles and some romance. I knew I had to tread carefully and tried to be understanding. Sadly, my son was poorly, so was harder to please and often wanted his mum. He was definitely more vocal and more handsome every time I saw him. Even though my son hadn't bonded with me, I had with him – it was special. I loved him so much, it really did hurt.

The next day didn't go the way I thought it would. It started out fine. His mum had even dressed him in one of the tops I had bought him – that was a nice touch. By lunchtime, he was flagging; he fell asleep in his buggy. His mum looked at me and said 'are you coming' as she made her way to her bedroom, undressing as she went. I didn't think anything would happen, considering how things had been the past few months. I certainly wasn't going to say no – not when it's the woman I loved. It was our son waking up that ended any more fun.

Then, just like that, it was time to go. I hated it and would have done anything to stay with my son and his mum. I knew that was a dream that wouldn't come true, even though there'd been progress. I was once again blinded by love and would find out the hard way exactly how she felt about me. I felt used and abused all over again. Everything was about to change, and all the beliefs that had kept me strong would come tumbling down like a house of cards.

I was dreading the journey back. I took the bus as it was cheaper; I'd spent a lot on Christmas presents. The journey down was the worst I'd ever had since my health problems began. Once we left Victoria Coach Station in London, the pain was so bad I was in tears and rocking backwards and forwards in agony. I then had to endure the rest of the journey, unable to take more pain relief. The return journey was only slightly more bearable but still took a lot out of me.

It took me two days to get over it before I could stand properly, let alone walk straight. It was the longest it had taken me to get over any travelling. I was a mess and no good to anyone. I'd learnt the hard way that, even though I was devoted to my ex, she felt differently to me. A couple of times while visiting, my legs had given way, which had me almost collapsing, and all my ex could do was walk around me going silent, as though she either didn't know what to do or just didn't want to. Honestly, I have no idea why she reacted that way, but it did make me realise she wouldn't have coped when my health was at its worst.

It was six days after getting back when things went downhill again. It started out as little things – comments or reactions to what I would say. She was making it harder and harder. She made it clear how much control she had with me seeing my son. My hopes of having a special Christmas were rapidly fading!

The part that pushed my ex over the edge was completely innocent in my eyes. I asked her if she would take some photos on Christmas Day of our son and send them to me when she had the time. She wasn't happy about this, telling me how busy she would be and wouldn't get time to send them to me. For some reason, she didn't listen to the part about sending them whenever. This turned into an argument that was impossible for me to win. In the end, I just left it and hoped she would do this one thing for me. I never asked for anything prior to that.

I was looking forward to Boxing Day. I was due to speak to my son. It was meant to be special, but the lead-up to it was uncomfortable. Christmas Day evening, my phone kept saying that a message was trying to come through. I guessed it was my ex trying to send photos, but for whatever reason, nothing came through.

Boxing Day came, and though I was excited at hearing my son's voice, I was nervous about how his mum was going to be. Straight away she asked what I thought of the photos. I told her I never received them. I asked if she could send them again. She said she tried once and wouldn't again, so tough. Then followed an argument. I quickly got her to put our son on before somebody said something they couldn't come back from. The conversation was short, but hearing my son's voice was enough.

When his mum came back on the phone, she was short with me, and the call ended with neither of us happy. I hoped that if I left her alone for a couple of weeks, she would have calmed down and made peace before my son's birthday. I was walking a tightrope that was so slim it wouldn't take much to snap – but snap it did.

January 2014 was a tough month. As my son's birthday grew nearer, his mum and I grew further apart. The arguments were more regular, like when we lived together, except this time I wasn't taking it on the chin no more. I grew tired of the "yes miss, no miss, three bags full miss." I'd had my fair share of being taken advantage of, and now it was time I stood up for myself. Through all the bad words and nastiness, it was time I got something. I told her it was time she started being fair and stopped treating me like I was nothing. This, of course, didn't go down well. She made it clear I wasn't allowed to see my son anytime soon.

I was stuck and didn't know what to do. In the end, I contacted the Citizens Advice Bureau for advice. Desperate times call for desperate measures. They told me that the first thing I needed to do was try mediation. It means we sit down together and talk in the hope we came to a reasonable agreement for both sides. I texted my ex and asked if she was willing to do mediation. She replied no. I showed the person at the C.A.B. and asked what my options were. They said the next step was to go to court to get my rights. It was then I realised how badly I'd screwed up. When my son was born and I first went to see a solicitor, I should have followed through. Suppose that's karma biting me on the arse.

February 2014, the day of my son's birthday. I'd had no contact with my ex for the previous two weeks. I hoped that by giving my ex time to calm down, we could find common ground and she'd let me see my son. It was a Sunday morning, so I texted a simple "Happy Birthday. Daddy loves you very much." I left it at that, but got no reply. It was later that afternoon I decided to take a chance by calling. I thought she would allow me to at least speak to my son. Instead, my ex's mum answered the call. As soon as she spoke, I knew it wasn't going to be a nice call. She laid into me, saying how I had ruined her daughter and because of me, she wasn't coping. I told her I just wanted to speak to my son. This is when I realised how much mother and daughter were alike. She said I couldn't speak to her. I told her I didn't want to talk to her, just my son, and again she said I couldn't speak to her. Back and forth this went for five minutes before I hung up on her. I was not happy and spent the next twenty minutes running the conversation over and over in my mind. In the end, I let my emotions get the better of me and texted, "If she can't cope, then who the hell is looking after my son?" Not my finest moment. There was no reply, and I would find out the hard way – she changed her number, cutting me off completely.

No social media, no mobile phone, nothing, and there wasn't a single thing I could do about it. Life can really suck sometimes, and I'd once again learned that believing there's good in someone can fail miserably.

I thought that if I gave her enough time, she would come running when she wanted money or something else from me. I was fooling myself. Some people said I was just used to produce a baby, but I knew that couldn't be true. I knew deep down there was a time when she did love me, but for whatever reason, I was just not good enough for her – which really hurt. I would love that woman for nearly twenty years and be left with a son I adored. In the end, she showed no sign of wanting to include me in his life. It's a battle that is far from over. It's taken me too many years to get it sorted, and eventually I will, if it's the last thing I do. She may have taken my self-worth and torn my heart out of my chest, but she can never take away the fact that boy is very much mine.

Chapter 49

I worked out a plan to take back control and be a father to my child. I'd had 8 days with my son and didn't want that to be the end of it. It seemed straightforward until I got into the nitty-gritty of it. I contacted Southampton's family court to find out what the process would be to get my father's rights. As my son lived in Southampton, that is where I would have to go. I had the law on my side in theory. I would need to apply for two things. First, a Parental Responsibility Order, which would give me legal rights as a father, and then a Visitation Order, which would give me access to my son. Sounded straightforward, but it wasn't. I would need a paternity test done to prove I am his father before any court appearance. Thankfully, I knew he was mine. I would then finally have a legal document saying I am a father.

The problem was that they would expect me to see my son at least once a month, which in theory was brilliant and much better than what I had through his mum, but I couldn't manage the travelling, especially regularly, and I couldn't afford it. Even though I was living with my parents, I wasn't rolling in money. I was trying to keep fit, but my health was getting worse. As the weeks turned into months, I realised my ex wasn't going to get in touch. I had one of two choices: 1) go all in and take my ex to court and be in my son's life straight away. The risk being my health would prevent me from making the journey. This could mean the courts would think I wasn't committed; my ex would use that as a way to stop me from seeing him. Option 2 was to wait it out, hope I can get a place of my own, and eventually move much nearer. I was willing to make sacrifices to be there for my son.

I quickly realised that option 2 was my only option. My son was young enough that he wouldn't remember me anyway. It was so hard telling myself that I was doing the right thing for my son's benefit. Regardless of how much it hurt, I had to be patient. I had no idea back then how hard that decision would be and the ramifications for waiting so long. I didn't know how quickly I'd get my own place or if I could move nearer.

Getting my own place was proving much harder than I thought. The fact that I was a single male with no known dependents meant I was bottom of the list. It would take letters from my GP and regular phone calls to get the message across – that falling up and down stairs was worrying when you have metal rods against your spine.

While all this was going on, I still volunteered in a charity shop until I was late twice and they fired me. I never knew that was a thing, but it turns out it is. It was worse by the fact that they were expecting too much from me, while management stood around yapping – no loss in the end. I decided to have a break for a couple of months and then went to a different charity shop. It was more relaxed, and a great group of people who never judged me or expected more than I could handle.

A couple of months after my son's birthday, I finally had enough and decided to stop going to church. I may not have been a full-on believer, but the faith I had went out the window when my ex blocked me from our son. But when so many things were going against me, I couldn't face church. I couldn't honestly say there was a God when I was being punished every single day. How could I continue thinking positively when everything that mattered to me – everything I loved–was taken from me when I tried to do everything right? My life had turned into a disaster; I had to make changes.

In May 2014, I bumped into the lass I tried it on with the night I proposed to my ex-wife. Anyway, we reconnected, and I made a big mistake. I understood what being on the rebound was – it never crossed my mind. I never dreamed I would fall victim to it, but I did – and big time.

It started out well, and I was actually feeling like there was hope for happiness. Even though she was very different from my type of woman, I thought that if I gave it time, it would work.

Then my health took a downward slide. I was taking so much pain medication; the side effects made me weaker. As a result, I found my legs giving out on me to the point I had to use my manual wheelchair when I went out. I took no joy in it, but had so little strength, and with the medication, I was a zombie most of the time. You take them to ease the pain, but end up with more problems. Sleeping was difficult, and when you do sleep, you struggle to stay awake. Your body has a mind of its own – even affects your toilet habits.

It took a long time, but I managed to come off some of the pain medication. I got to function more. The pain was just as bad, if not worse, but you find ways of balancing the good with the bad. Those rare days when you actually feel half-human, you make the most of it and push yourself, and then take it easy on the really bad days.

Back to the relationship – I was with her when my best mate Phil from Butlins got married, and she came with me. It wasn't until after the dust settled that even Phil said that we were not good for each other. The rebound thing proved true.

The irony with Phil – we both have sons and got with the mothers about the same time. My son was born nine days before his; the odds on that must be astronomical. The wedding itself was good fun. It was the first I'd been to since my own, and I got to meet some mutual friends Phil and I met online.

About a month after coming back, the relationship went down the toilet! It started with a benign argument – I've forgotten what it was about. All attempts to make peace were ignored, and promises to meet up were broken, until the good old 'it's over' by text message. I was upset at the time; I thought I liked her. It wasn't until months later, when I looked back, that I realised it should never have happened. I wasn't attracted to her and was still in love with my son's mother.

December 2014 was hard. It was the first anniversary since seeing my son, 5th December, to be exact. I still couldn't celebrate Christmas anyway, but after what happened the year before, it was even harder. I wasn't fun to be around; I'd shut myself away. It was harder on my mum – she loved Christmas! I got good at faking a smile when she was around. She saw right through me. She pretended that she didn't. She was a very special woman!

I don't know how I got through Christmas – it felt like one of the worst years of my life. Considering 12 months prior, it was so close to being the best year. Boxing Day was no better – a year since speaking to my son. Although I wasn't able to see my son, I still made sure I bought him a Christmas card and presents, and did the same for his birthday. I always hoped that it wouldn't be long until I got to give them to him. I also bought the mummy cards – for Christmas, Birthday and Mother's Day – out of principle. I wanted to show my son that even though his mum refused to acknowledge me as his father, I would not shirk my responsibilities. I was brought up to be a better man than that.

The hardest part was not knowing what my son was into and what he was like. I started buying clothes until I accepted he would have grown out of them long before I could give them to him.

In January 2015, my other best friend, Terry, was turning 40. He was having a birthday party and invited me down – I couldn't say yes quick enough. It had been nine and a half years since I was last in Bognor Regis. I'd never really had a reason to go down and didn't have the time before then. Although I was still working in the charity shop, I wasn't paid, so could take time off whenever I wanted.

I booked a B&B just outside Bognor town centre. It was round the corner from where I lived in 2004–2005, the same road my friend Terry lived on, which worked out pretty good for me. I was actually excited – not only was it a holiday of sorts, but I was back where I felt at home. The journey down was interesting. I took the train and had my own wheels. A few months prior, my dad found a mobility scooter for sale and bought it to help me out. I'd never even considered getting one, but it was a lifesaver some days. The only downside being, it was second-hand and the battery never lasted long. A couple of times I got caught out with a dead battery and had to wheel it home.

I got there on the Friday afternoon and booked for the weekend. As soon as I came out of the railway station, I just stood there and took it all in – I was home! I felt a wave of peace wash over me, and I smiled for the first time in a long time. I was where I belonged. I was where my dearest friends were. I was where I had happy memories. And I was where I needed to be.

Once I'd found the B&B and got settled in, I went out to my old road to see my friend for the first time in nine years. I also got to meet his partner and two youngest sons for the first time. We hugged in the most manly way possible, and then he introduced me to everyone. They made me feel welcome. I got to visit the parts of Bognor I enjoy the most.

I'd also been in touch with my friend Tracy; we had arranged to meet on the Sunday, which would give me the chance to meet her 2 sons for the first time. A busy weekend seeing friends — I needed it after being in a bad place for far too long.

Even though it was winter and cold out, it didn't spoil it for me. I always found the sea more exciting during stormy times — the rougher the better. I'm easily pleased. That night I went to my chippy: sausage and chips, simple but filling. I certainly slept well that night; travelling always took it out of me. The health problems made it worse; sleep is important to aid recovery.

Saturday I spent the day on my typical walk around, taking it all in and seeing what had changed since I was last down. Apart from the usual different shops, it was mostly the same. I could have relaxed in the B&B but wanted to make the most of my time down. The room was nice: there was a single bed, a bedside cabinet, a wardrobe, tea and coffee making facilities, and a small TV that had a poor connection. It was also en-suite, with a shower that I had to step up to. The step wasn't small, so not always easy to get in. There was a restaurant area for breakfast; next to that, a door that led to a lounge.

There was a bar area with comfortable sofas, with a choice of books and DVDs for anyone who wanted to watch a movie. It backed onto a room with a pool table and the back garden.

The garden was big and had a nice covered area, ideal for smokers.

The evening of the party, I wore a nice shirt and smart trousers. It was quite a journey to the venue but good exercise. I was glad to get there and get my first drink. Although I was on a lot of pain medication, I could still have a drink—it never caused me any issues.

There was a great turn-out. I was so pleased for my friend that many made the effort. I got to meet people I'd only heard about, and a couple I already knew from my days at Butlins. It was a good night, and my mate had a great time. I didn't drink much; I don't need to drink a lot to enjoy myself. I was still glad to get to bed that night.

Sunday, I woke up bright and early and enjoyed a nice English breakfast. A fry-up for breakfast always tastes better when staying in a B&B or a hotel. I had a busy day ahead, so needed all the energy I could get. It was early afternoon when I met Tracy and her family. I was excited—I'd met her husband years earlier. We hugged, and even though it had been a decade, we were happy to see each other. Her boys were adorable and very polite. We went to the Brewers Fayre pub, which ironically was where I last worked in Bognor. I'd taken my mobility scooter, which her boys loved, particularly the eldest, who was eager to have a go on it. I got him to stand where I put my feet while I sat in the seat, and we both used the accelerator to make sure I could take over if something went wrong. He had great fun.

We spent a couple of hours chatting and laughing. It was a perfect afternoon and finished the weekend off a treat. It was bittersweet saying goodbye. What I didn't anticipate was how far I'd travelled — the scooter battery died on my way back to the B&B.

I couldn't believe my luck; I was over 100 metres away and on the wrong side of the road. I couldn't exactly call a taxi, so I put the scooter into neutral and used it like a skateboard, using my feet to move it along whilst sitting down. All I needed was pedals to look like Fred Flintstone. I was worn out when I got back and charging in the restaurant.

I'd picked up some snacks from the shop on my way back, so didn't need to go out again for food, and then spent the rest of the day taking it easy. I knew I'd need an early night for the journey home.

After another unhealthy but very filling breakfast, I was ready to leave. The scooter had been charging all night and was ready to go. The owners of the B&B were an older couple and very nice — I knew that I'd go back sometime. They made me feel welcome the whole time I was there. I got to the railway station. Once on the train, I was looking forward to getting home.

In London, I needed to change stations to make it to Cambridge. Usually, I would have used the underground, but with the scooter that wasn't possible, so I had to use a taxi. The way down was a nightmare trying to get the scooter into a London taxi, but on the way back it was easier. I was home late afternoon and was well and truly shattered.

After a text message to my best mate to say I was home, I was ready for something to eat and an early night. The holiday may have been over, but the effects on my body would last for days. Recovery took far too long. I couldn't spend the rest of my life sitting around never doing anything — somehow I had to learn to suck it up and get on with it.

That was the only excitement of that year. The usual struggle on my son's birthday a week after getting back home. He was 2 and hard to comprehend — all the things he was able to say and do, and walking properly. So much I'd missed — it broke my heart a little more each day. I knew it was my burden to carry, but it didn't mean I liked it. But life goes on. The year was filled with more days in pain than not. Trouble sleeping, and when I did sleep, I struggled to wake up — it felt like a never-ending nightmare. I was finding it harder to do steps. It was hard lifting my legs properly.

I tried to see the positives. I thought back to when I had my first back operation, when the consultant told me that if the vertebrae slipped further, I could have been paralysed from the waist down. There were some days I wished that I didn't feel the pain. Then I'd remember the other parts — permanently in a wheelchair, a bag to go to the toilet, and never being able to have sex again — and decided the pain meant I was alive.

Yes, at times I was in so much pain I just wanted to crawl into a ball and cry, but I was alive. Yes, I couldn't work, and even the volunteering was getting too much, but I was alive. Yes, I felt like I could never find happiness with a woman as my confidence was non-existent, but I was alive. Yes, I hated my life and what I'd become, but I was alive. Yes, everything that had made me who I was had slipped through my fingers, but I was still alive. Yes, I was still alive, and for that I was grateful.

December — the memories of seeing my son last flooded my mind. In one hand I felt joy for the time I got with him and the memories. At the same time, the depression got worse — all I wanted was to be a dad to my son. I still loved his mum, and as every day passed, I felt further away from them. I couldn't escape — we created a child with love.

Every day I would hold my mobile phone close, hoping beyond hope that it would ring and my ex would tell me she was sorry. Every child needs to have both parents in their life. I was still a fool, but when you love someone so much, you'll believe anything. They don't call them dreams for nothing, but when you wake up, reality is very different.

The second Christmas came and went, and I tried so hard to smile for my mum's sake. She knew how hard I tried, and knew there was nothing she or anyone else could say. It wasn't a complete wash. I had a random friend request on Facebook. It was a guest I met back in 2000, Bev, a sweetheart. She reminded me of a younger me when we met, as she was quiet. By the time I'd met her, I'd come out of my shell. We met in Jaks one night and chatted. I was just shocked she remembered me, let alone my name. I must have made her laugh, something I was good at. It was nice catching up and finding out what she had been up to. We have remained friends ever since.

Chapter 50

A new year, it was 2016. I didn't hold much hope. I was in for a surprise. It started with a new set of wheels. My mobility scooter was on its last legs; it was time for an upgrade. I was still living with my parents with no sign of changing. I was on the full-rate mobility with my Disability Living Allowance benefit. I'd already received a booklet about mobility scooters and cars. I wanted a car; I figured that would give me the best long-term relief from walking. The problem was I'd never learnt to drive. They told me I'd need someone with a full driving licence to go on the insurance. Part of the package, I could get lessons to learn to drive. All seemed straightforward. I asked my dad, with the reassurance that if anything happened, it would still fall on me.

I'd been to the local Vauxhall garage and had a look at a couple of cars and felt like I knew which was right. All I had to do was to start the paperwork, and then I'd finally start to drive. Then my dad decided that he didn't want to go on the insurance and left me up a creek without a paddle. I had nobody I could ask, so my dream came crashing down. Instead, I got a new mobility scooter instead. It would mean I wouldn't lose as much money but still have more freedom. I opted to have the cheaper all-weather canopy. I thought I was being smart. I was very wrong.

I'd had the scooter a couple of months before I found out how much of a liability the canopy could be. For one, I couldn't use the scooter when it was windy, as the canopy made it top-heavy and could blow over. Mind you, the advantage when it rained was a benefit. I soon noticed that being 37 and using a mobility scooter did not endear me to the general public. The dirty looks I got started to make me paranoid. It didn't matter if they were young, old, male or female – they all gave me dirty looks. It was horrible. I even started to wonder if I should use one at all. Those days, I could barely walk straight. Even with crutches, I knew it was a necessity for me.

You learn a lot about people when you're at your worst! The only thing that kept me going was my Butlins friends. I always had their support through thick and thin, good and bad. There were many times when I felt low and dejected with my life, and all I had to do was to call or message them, and I'd feel like I mattered again. They were my lifeline. I would have been lost without them.

The one that really came through for me was Janelle. We had remained close over the years and would regularly chat for hours. One of those long conversations, she suggested going to

Butlins for a holiday. I jumped at the chance. She said she would arrange it all, and I would give her the money – so that is what we did. She booked a Monday–Friday break a week before half-term. It would be my first time back at Butlins in 12 years. I couldn't wait.

Even though I'd been classed as disabled for a few years, I had never made the most of what was available to me apart from my bus pass. I got it for being profoundly deaf; it didn't count in that context. I got a disabled rail pass that gave me a third off all rail travel for one year for £20. I'd agreed to meet Janelle in Bognor Regis. I hadn't seen her since my wedding 11 years prior. I was as much excited about seeing her as I was the holiday.

The journey was easier than the last one 15 months prior. It helped it wasn't as far, and the destination was my happy place. Either way, I was in good spirits. I made it to Bognor Regis before Janelle – but only just.

When she arrived, we hugged. We decided to walk to Butlins and take it slowly; we were on holiday, after all. We chatted almost like we hadn't been in regular contact. We never run out of things to say.

We had a unique bond – more like brother and sister than just friends – so much so we had no problem sharing a room. We had a knack for talking endlessly, and no subject was off-limits. It is a rare gift to find a friend like that of the opposite sex.

I knew Butlins had changed over the years but didn't realise how much. I lived in Bognor Regis when they built the first hotel; they've since added two more. They looked amazing from the outside, but more impressive up close. I'd never stayed in a hotel before, and that is exactly where we were booked – the Shoreline Hotel, the one I saw being built.

I was in for some new experiences; it had changed so much. Back in the day, redcoats would be stationed in the Skyline Pavilion with a set-out area to welcome the new guests and hand out the welcome packs with keys for your room. But being in a hotel, we had to go to the reception of that hotel to collect everything.

Our room was easy to find once we got out of the lift. It was a straightforward twin room – perfect for us. There was a nicely laid-out bathroom with toilet, sink and bath with shower facilities that suited me. The window backed onto the play area between the hotel and the edge of the building that housed Centre Stage. That was about all that was familiar on the outside. Where the old arcade used to be was now an American restaurant. Next to that, where there used to be stairs to the entrance to the snooker hall, was now the entrance to a conference centre. The one thing that stuck out the most was the greenery everywhere.

When I worked there, they had a lot of open areas between the buildings; it made for easy access. But Butlins had taken a greener approach, and there were bushes that went down the middle of the walkways and were like that around most of the resort. For an old timer, it was surreal and didn't feel right, but that's progress, I suppose.

Once we settled into our room and got freshened up, we decided to go for the grand tour. We knew some of the changes from the Butlins website, like the different restaurants, but going around we were both shocked. For instance, our old restaurant, Ocean Drive, was still there, but rather than one big and one little restaurant, it was split into three separate restaurants with three different names and styles. That was the hardest change; I had many fond memories working in Ocean Drive and made many friends. It was a special place — ask anyone who worked around that time, they would agree.

The second evening, our old friend Tony, who was back working on site, got us into Coral Beach restaurant for dinner. This was also different from the old waitered one. It was more like the old Ocean Drive, being self-service. Then it was spoilt!

An Eastern European member of staff did a birthday shout. I so badly wanted to stand up and show him how it was done. Even Janelle and Tony said it was poor. It wasn't his accent, and definitely not his English, which was very good — it was the vibe. He sounded like a robot reading a script; there was no emotion and certainly no individuality to it. To us oldies, it just wasn't the same. We made it special, and there was no table set up like we used to do. It kind of burst the bubble of being back. It was still the Butlins that made me who I was and had the same sounds and smells, but the changes spoiled some of my memories that were so ingrained in my soul.

I realised that living in the past is great when reminiscing with friends, but being back was a whole different experience. I had to move forwards like Butlins did — it was harder than I thought it would be.

It wasn't all bad. I made a fool of myself, which gave Janelle and Tony a good laugh. They had one of those extra-large deck chairs, which I jumped in. Big mistake! I soon learned what it was like when a turtle is on its back and unable to turn over. Looking back, I could see the funny side, but at the time I had my friends laughing so hard they were almost in tears while I'm stuck like a beached whale. Eventually, they helped me out.

The only real downside about that week was the weather — it was windy and rained a lot. Although usually I'd love to be down the beach, I lacked the energy; it was more difficult than I thought it would be. We did go to the beach one night and had a nice stroll along the promenade. It was nice, as I showed her where I used to go to be alone — the same place that January 2002 I went after my Grandad had passed and threw my poppy out to sea. It wasn't all about what I wanted to do or go; Janelle had her places too. We walked into town one day to have a mooch and see how much it changed. Even though it was only 15 months since I'd last seen it, it had been 14 years for Janelle.

It was a nice break. The resort was quiet and had virtually no nightlife. Jaks was still there, and we were determined to go one evening, hoping to recapture some of the old magic. We were in for disappointment. It was so quiet at 11:00 p.m., with less than 20 people including the staff. The music was done by a DJ on the main stage, not next to the bar in a booth like it once was. There was no atmosphere at all. One good thing — they still served a lot of the same drinks that we once drank, like the VK orange and passion fruit and WKD varieties. Alcopops are great if you want to drink and not worry about getting drunk quickly. We only had a couple of drinks, as they closed not long after midnight. That was the last time I went to Jaks, as they closed it for good. Anyone who had worked or visited Butlins at the turn of the century through to the 2010s would have experienced that place and probably feel the same loss that we did. A true end of an era!

We did catch a couple of shows while there, but they were all aimed at young children and families — same as the Skyline at night, when there was virtually nobody about. Our day was very different. In Centre Stage, they had their rollover hotdog stand — we had them back in 1999 — they still smelled just as good. Had to have one while I was there.

Our last night, we opted to try out the American restaurant, as it was opposite our hotel. It was as you'd expect. The music was pleasant, and the staff were mostly women and all with smiles, which was a far cry from the other restaurants. It was refreshing, and the food was good — just what we needed for a last meal on resort.

It was great catching up with Janelle in person, even talking one night until dawn. I got the chance to meet up with my best mate Terry one evening. It was much needed for us both. Janelle and I had plenty of laughs, which was great. I could still make a woman laugh without dropping my pants — so, result there. I'd done more in those few days than I had in three years — I amazed myself. I'd pay for it afterwards.

We walked to the railway station and said our farewells, with promises to message each other when we got home. We got on our separate trains and left Bognor Regis. Neither of us knew when we would see each other again in person, or where our lives were going, but we knew our friendship was as strong as it had ever been. We both had changes on the horizon.

Chapter 51

I was relieved to be home; Bognor will always be close to my heart. The journey wasn't too bad, except the underground, which is horrible on crutches. You'd be amazed how rude people can be to disabled people. Very few people in general pay attention to someone with mobility issues.

When out on crutches, people are so rude, but mothers with pushchairs are the worst. But, down the pub, drunk people or those on the way to being drunk are the nicest people. They open doors, let you pass and even make room for you at the bar. Obviously, this is all personal experience, and I am not tarnishing everyone with the same brush; sometimes, though, it's hard not to judge after 10-plus years on crutches.

As May ended, June came with a new beginning. For three and a half years, I'd done everything possible to get a ground floor flat or a bungalow. I was calling the housing people almost weekly. Every month, there was a list with properties available in the area.

It was on the internet, and you'd bid for them. I lost count of how many times I bid and never heard anything. It was disheartening. That was until that June when I got a phone call about a property that would be ready in a few weeks. Would I be interested in viewing it? It didn't take me long to say, "Yes, please!"

It had been far too long since I had something to look forward to. Finally, my time had come. I didn't know what to expect and had never been to where the flat was located. Having the mobility scooter helped, not just for getting there but to validate needing my own place. I arrived ten minutes early. I didn't have to wait long before the lady arrived. She told me she was showing the flat opposite to an older lady, then she would show me the flat I was there to see. The other lady arrived for the other flat and was in and out in no time. I thought that either it was a tiny flat or she wasn't happy. It turned out it wasn't big enough for her. Then it was my turn. She took me into the flat and explained that it still needed more work and wouldn't be ready for 2–3 weeks, which to me was fine, as I would need time to get packed and arrange a man with a van.

Walking into the flat, I felt a mixture of anticipation and excitement. I was under no illusions that the first property I visited would be the right one, but I needed it and hoped for first-time lucky. I needed some luck, and my ultimate plan depended on me getting my own place. Once I'd been in a property a year, I could then apply for a transfer to another town. Ideally, it would be Bognor Regis, so I was nearer to my son and around my friends. It sounded simple on paper, but was far from it.

The flat was a good size and looked big enough for me. I'd only need it for a year, give or take. The one problem with the flat was the garden. It was small and all paving slabs, but the back gate had steps up to it. I wouldn't be able to put my mobility scooter round there. I figured that I could find a way to make it work. Then I had a lightbulb moment and asked the lady about the other flat. She said I could have a look while I was there. It was a similar shape but slightly bigger. The airing cupboard was huge. It also had a wet room, which would be a massive help, especially on the days my mobility was bad. I would have loved a carpeted bathroom with a shower stall, but you can't have it all.

Overall, the flat was perfect and was only half a mile down the road from my parents' home. The lady said that if I wanted that flat, I would have to tell her there and then and sign the paperwork. As it was ready, I would have to move in straight away. I took a few deep breaths and had another look round just to be sure and said, "Yes, I'll take it."

I did it. I finally had my independence back! It felt as though a huge weight had lifted off my shoulders, and I could breathe again. Once the nitty-gritty was taken care of and the paperwork completed, I could say it was mine. I waited until the lady left and then called my mum and told her. She was happy for me, but I knew she was going to miss me. I spent the next 10 minutes just taking it all in and planning in my mind how I was going to get set. Although they said it was ready to move in, there was still a lot of work to do. I had to wait for the forms from Dulux so I could order the paint I'd been allocated, so I could decorate. I suddenly realised how much I needed to do, and the elation had turned to worry.

I made contact with the town council to get the ball rolling on housing benefit and council tax. I made an appointment with my bank to sort out contents insurance. I was not taking any risks that would leave me unable to replace anything. Then I went to my local Hughes to see about renting a washing machine and a cooker. I didn't have the money to buy brand new, and at least with renting, I'm covered if there were problems. All this I did in the first few days after getting the keys. The one thing that I didn't foresee was that to qualify for the housing benefit, I would need to be sleeping there straight away. I got the keys on the Thursday and somehow had to get a man and a van by the Sunday. I was able to use my scooter to at least take a few bits to the flat, like a stereo and, of course, a kettle – can't start the day without a cuppa.

After two trips back and forth, I realised how out of shape I was. I was going to need money to start over. I'd need carpet, as all the floors were concrete, and carpet isn't cheap. I didn't fancy wood flooring. It did become clear how much easier it had been when I moved to Bognor Regis in 2004 – it was already furnished, and I took out a loan before moving. But when you're on your own, it's very different. When it comes to all the amenities like gas, electric, water, landline, internet, and TV licence, there were a lot of decisions to make. The biggest shock was still to come.

I managed to get a van sorted for the Sunday and had a couple of friends come round to help load and unload the van. I was grateful for the help – I needed it. The only problem was the van driver decided to double-book and was only willing to do one trip when I needed two. The rest had to be done between two cars. It was frustrating and time-consuming, but we eventually got it done. The funniest part was watching my dad not only help but move quicker than I'd seen him move in years. Then it clicked – he was making sure I was gone.

I'd always had an uncomfortable relationship with my dad. He was never the loving type and certainly never embraced his children. His excuse was, 'I never had the best teacher,' as his dad had a hard life and was old school. Seen but not heard and all that, he was the boss. He was in the army during the Second World War in one of the harshest and most dangerous places. It probably left him with psychological scars but he never spoke about it. We would tell our dad that just because he didn't have the most loving upbringing doesn't mean he had to be the same. Being one of three children was tough. When one of us was playing up, my dad would smack us all and say, 'Least I got the right one,' and we resented him for that. I made a pact; the day I became a father that I'd be nothing like my dad, and I'm proud to say that I'm not. I've only had a handful of days' experience, but my ex could never say I was a bad father to our child.

Living with my parents after that split had been hard. I have always been close with my mum and felt I could always talk to her about anything and everything. When her health got so bad she struggled to do most things, I was happy to help. When my own health got bad, I turned to my mum for support and advice as she understood. My dad never tried to understand. The bond I shared with my mum was priceless.

One night my mum was in a lot of pain. It started in her face and she had a headache, so I stayed up with her all night making sure she had fresh drinks and was comfortable. I didn't think too much about what was wrong; I kicked myself later. She didn't get better throughout the day, so I went with her to her

GP and that was when we found out she had a minor heart attack. An ambulance was promptly called. While we waited, I had to call my dad and my sister so they could get there in time. I was most annoyed at myself as I'd done first aid training only a few years earlier and didn't spot the signs. Then again, there were no traditional heart attack symptoms. I kept apologising to my mum, but she would always say it was fine and I couldn't have known. I felt guilty for a long time after. It wasn't a bad one, although she already had heart disease. My dad never had the patience to help my mum and never would have stayed up all night with his own wife if she needed it. Hard not to compare yourself to the ones that came before you.

Even when I was married, my ex-wife had minor knee surgery and didn't cope with it at all well (she couldn't handle any pain). Before I left for work, I made sure she had drinks, food, TV remote and anything else she may need. My mum always said I should have been a carer, as I have a caring nature and am happy to help. Problem is, I get attached too easily and it would tear me apart when someone died.

Back to the story. I had all my belongings in my flat and now had to work out where to put it. Fun times! I knew I couldn't do too much as I would need to move all the furniture for painting and the carpet being laid. My priority was getting the fridge and freezer plugged in and then my bed set up. I'd been sleeping on a 2-seater sofa for a few nights and was looking forward to a proper bed. Mind you, I've slept on much worse.

Once I got my TV set up, I had a problem — no aerial. No Freeview, no nothing — bugger! Luckily, I had a lot of DVDs and was able to watch them at my leisure. There wasn't a lot that I missed on TV and I hated soaps, so could have been worse. I did have a Now TV box, but again I was limited on what to watch. When I went to Hughes to arrange renting a washing machine and cooker, I had a look at TV packages. I'd already had a look at BT for phone line and internet and, before I'd made a decision, I saw a deal for Sky that worked out the same price as BT but with TV included — a no-brainer. I'd already tried a Freeview box but it didn't work.

A few days after I'd moved all my belongings in, the paint arrived and the hard work began. It was the middle of June and very warm out — so much so I had to paint while in my under-wear and wearing a protector over the top to avoid ending up smothered in paint. My bedroom I managed to paint in a day, but the living room took two and, by the time it was done, I was well and truly shattered. I left doing the hall until the following year.

Getting carpet, I made a fatal mistake; I'd had a quote from a local store which included free underlay but waited until I went to Bury St Edmunds to find something cheaper. That is what I did and have regretted it ever since. I was offered a stick-down carpet which worked out at over £150 cheaper, and it really is true — you get what you pay for. The guys that fitted it did a poor job; there were gaps up at the wall and the quality was terrible. Cleaning it is impossible. Whenever something got spilt on it, 99% of the time it wouldn't come up no matter what I used. Least I wasn't walking on cement floors anymore.

Once all that was done and I'd bought net curtains and curtains, I felt ready to open my doors to friends and have a housewarming. It was set for a Saturday afternoon/evening mid-July. I already met some of my neighbours, one of which I actually knew, and invited a couple of them. When the day came, I'd gotten the booze ready and waited and waited and waited. The neighbour I knew popped round but had to go back because a thunderstorm had started and he had to see to his dogs. Then I got the messages apologising that they couldn't make it. I was gutted. Getting my own place after waiting so long was a big deal to me and I wanted to share it. I was getting used to being let down. I know people have lives of their own, but it would have been nice for a few to pop round even for an hour, but I guess it wasn't meant to be.

Another thing I'd always longed for was a garden of my own. Just sucked that when I finally got it, I was disabled. The worst being bending — for a short time was agony. The one thing you need most when gardening — yeah, bending over. My front garden was the only one with soil but was a mess of weeds. A friend agreed to help dig it over. He helped with the compost and some planting too. I hated to ask for help, but there was no way I had it in me to do it. I would need his help again once more a few months later.

Since then, I've maintained it myself even when it's left me barely able to stand. The back garden was a different matter. First of all, I needed some furniture so I could enjoy it. Then getting pots and spending a fortune to get it set up how I wanted — it was worth it.

I also invested in bird feeders. Growing up, my mum fed the birds and I wanted to continue her tradition. It didn't take long to attract them, as where I live isn't far from a wildlife sanctuary of sorts. It would take time to see all the varieties of birds in the area. I've been shocked at how many.

Then came the first big obstacle: I'd been under the hospital for a painful bunion on my right foot. I was booked in for surgery a few months after moving into my flat.

This time, it would be done in day surgery – a big difference from my left bunion surgery in 2011. Having the mobility scooter was a godsend. The first two weeks I had to keep my foot raised and rested. I was too independent to rely on anyone to pick up shopping.

Prior to the surgery, I'd been on the go non-stop and managed to lose some weight; I was proud of myself for that. After the six weeks were up and I could remove the protective shoe I had to wear, I found out the weight I'd lost was back with interest.

Before I knew it, Christmas was fast approaching. I decided to go all out decorating my flat. I still struggled mentally and emotionally because I couldn't share it with my son, but I had to keep going. I even put my tree up and went mad on making it look the best I possibly could.

A couple of days before Christmas, I had been round to my parents'. I still visited them regularly, making sure my mum was okay. It had been a pleasant evening and I didn't leave until after 9:00 p.m. As my scooter was road legal and had headlights,

I took the main road, going the maximum 8 mph. I had my fairy lights inside the all-weather canopy, making me easier to see.

All was good until I reached the T-junction between my parents' housing estate and the housing estate where I lived. When a car approached the junction, I knew I had right of way. That was when I realised the car wasn't stopping and pulled out in front of me. Only my quick reactions saved me from a nasty accident as I swerved out the way. It was a Smart car, which was the exact same size as my scooter with the canopy. There was no way they couldn't have seen me.

Somehow, I made it home. Once the shaking had eased, I called the police to report it, fully aware there was nothing they could do. I didn't get the registration number and there were no cameras anywhere. I had no faith in the police after bad experiences. Doesn't matter how road safe you try to be – there are still idiots who think the world revolves around them.

After the failure of my housewarming, I decided to have another try for New Year's Day. But sadly, it went one step worse than last time with no visitors. You can't win them all, and I decided I wouldn't bother again.

Another year had passed and now it was 2017. I was excited at the prospect of reaching a year in my flat – then I could apply for a transfer. The early part of the year was pretty quiet, apart from issues with my mobility scooter. I found the poor pavements played havoc with the bracket that held the all-weather frame. I'd already had three broken frames in the year that I'd had it. The next one would be the funniest.

It was on a bank holiday Monday and I was about a quarter of a mile away from my flat, which was all uphill. I had no way of holding the frame up and driving home and couldn't call a taxi. I only had one option – call out a breakdown service. Yes, for a mobility scooter. Once I got through to the right person, all I could do was sit and wait. When it arrived, it was a full-length flatbed lorry. I was so embarrassed. The guy was polite and friendly, and we had a laugh at the absurdity of the situation. Once he got the whole scooter onto the back, I took my crutches and made the slow walk back uphill. He was patiently waiting for when I got back and helped me get the scooter to my flat.

That would be the last time it would happen. I came to an agreement with the Motability team to end my contract early. I was getting sick of the dirty looks off so many people and tired of canopy brackets breaking. It was time to get some control of my life again.

It worked out that, had I not ended the contract, I would have had it taken off me anyway – thanks to the moronic lackeys the government had used for assessments.

Early 2017, my Disability Living Allowance (DLA) was ending and I had to go onto the Personal Independent Payment (PIP). I'd done all the paperwork the right way and felt that I wouldn't have any problems. That was until the assessment! I went down in my mobility scooter and on my own – which went against me. The guy that did the assessment was a trained physiotherapist – at least, that is what he told me – but essentially, an idiot that didn't care about the job he was tasked with doing.

It was clear how bad my mobility was and the pain I was in. This included the constant flinching and inability to sit still, but he basically made out that I had no issues with my mobility and I was denied that part of the benefit. I was not happy – it was a lot of money to lose, and although I'd have given anything to have been able to work and earn a living, I couldn't change my circumstances.

It hit me hard and I challenged the decision more than once, and each time they denied me; it didn't help my mental state of mind. It would take three years before I finally got awarded the mobility element. I didn't get any back pay either.

The whole system is so bad that those who deserve it have to fight with everything they have. Then they break. There is a very high rate of suicide when it comes to being let down by the benefits system. I was lucky and just about managed to hold on with help until I finally got it sorted.

There is no pride in being on benefits, but we shouldn't be punished for not being able to work. I tried with the volunteering for three and a half years, and if I couldn't manage that, then there was no chance I'd manage a paid job. Common sense seems to have disappeared nowadays.

Chapter 52

I was back under the hospital, but this time for my right shoulder; it was 2018. Every time I reached out, my right arm would crack and I wouldn't be able to keep it raised. When you're right-handed and dependent on that arm, it makes any job a nightmare. I'd been in my flat a year, and my dreams of a transfer were lost. I was in a housing association flat; I couldn't put in for a transfer through them as they didn't have any properties where I wanted to go. I spoke to the council, and they said there was nothing they could do; I was out of options. The only thing I could do was to bide my time and hope my luck changed.

I was booked in for my shoulder surgery early summer – here we go again. I was having an arthroscopy by keyhole surgery. They make two incisions – one at the top of the shoulder and one at the front – and through these they scrape out the joint. In doing so, the arthritis eases a touch, and there is nothing blocking the joint's movement. Least that's what's meant to happen. This time, though, it worked. As part of the procedure, they have to numb the arm, which leaves it floppy, like you've slept on it funny. A mate said to me not to waste it, as it would feel like someone else doing it. I don't think I need to spell out what he meant. I didn't, though. I needed a sling for a couple of days to give the shoulder a chance to heal.

At the follow-up appointment, the consultant was happy with the result, and it's generally been good since. A few niggles here and there, but with arthritis that's expected.

The rest of the year was unremarkable. I was getting used to being on crutches all the time without the scooter. In some respects, it felt good to be upright most of the time. There were some scary moments when my legs gave way – I ended up on the floor. It seemed to happen at home, but I escaped permanent damage. The one thing that kept me going was my friends, particularly my Butlins friends. You can see why Butlins had been so important to me – those friends weren't just friends; they were the people that made life better just for being there.

One thing that had helped was my neighbours upstairs – a husband and wife. When I struggled to take my wheelie bin out or bring it in, they would do it for me, and I'd often chat to them. Most of my neighbours were good people and polite – that is rare. I may not have chatted to all of them, but the ones I did, I got on well with. It wasn't a bad place to live. It did help that my direct neighbours were deaf – some more than me – but I always tried to be respectful with my noise day and night.

That Christmas, the depression hit me hard. I didn't decorate that year. I kept to myself mostly, except Christmas Day. We usually all got together at my parents' house, as my mum loved Christmas. My dad would cook – well, he would try. Even after years of doing it, you needed an iron stomach. It was never great, and somehow he never remembered what we liked to eat. That year, I made an appearance along with my sister to try and give my mum the best Christmas we could.

New Year wasn't any better. I did go out for a drink, but as per usual, the only thing I was able to pull was a muscle. I found that even though people were more respectful, the women still avoided me like the plague. Believe it or not, men are just as sensitive to rejection as women – we just hide it.

Another year gone, and no closer to where I wanted to be. The only good thing was spending time with my mum; her health was getting worse. We had an unwritten agreement that every night I would call – usually after midnight. We'd chat for ages; it was to make sure she made it into bed. She had a bad habit of falling asleep in her wheelchair – we feared she would fall out and seriously hurt herself. Our worst fears would come to pass.

I needed my own place and my independence, but I couldn't help feeling guilty I wasn't there for my mum.

Regardless of how bad my day was or how much pain I was in, I still worried about her more than myself. We were grateful for the time we got with her, but feared her time would come sooner rather than later. When something happened, our dad would rarely help her. One day in 2019, she woke up feeling unwell, so stayed in bed. I didn't visit until late afternoon, and she was comatose. It was scary, and my sister arrived just after me. We both had a go at our dad for doing nothing. We called an ambulance. When the paramedics arrived, she was no better. She spent a few days in hospital. We never found out why she was unwell.

Then, late summer, an avoidable accident shook us all up. My parents had been out for the day. My dad had left my mum in her wheelchair while he put the car in the garage. She was in the parking area, and one of the neighbor's ex-partners walked past her to his car. He wasn't paying attention as he reversed out of the parking space and, like a moth to a flame, drove straight into my mum, knocking her out of the wheelchair. It was bad. The ambulance was called and arrived quickly. She suffered a serious head wound, which bled a lot, and suffered various bruising. She was on blood thinners, which didn't help. After head scans and other checks, they kept her in overnight to monitor her, and then sent her home the next day. The psychological side-effects were awful; it kept her up at night and added more misery. Although the guy in the car was apologetic and devastated, he was lucky it wasn't worse. My mum forgave him – she was special like that.

Autumn 2019, I had reason to be excited. My good friend Terry came up for a few days. I had a nice sofa to sleep on, so had no problem giving up my bed. More than that, I was looking forward to some quality time with a dear friend. He had been a lifesaver during those hard days. He was looking forward to meeting my mum, as they had spoken over the years. My mum always welcomed our friends or partners, regardless of her true feelings. Case in point: my ex-wife. She knew she was bad news and not good for me, but kept quiet so I could learn – albeit the hard way. But, saying that, she had a great spirit and a wicked sense of humour. She and Terry hit it off. Although he only spent one afternoon with her, it was a good day.

Terry was due to spend a few days at mine, but due to unforeseen circumstances had to get back to his family early. It was a shame that it didn't last longer, but I appreciated seeing him. Talking on the phone is great, but sometimes you need that face-to-face. When he left, I realised how lucky I was to have such good friends. All of my dearest friends are from Butlins. I have other friends, but none share the same history or had the same experiences.

Then came 2020, and we all know how bad that year was. It didn't take a genius to work out a lockdown was fast approaching. I still visited my parents regularly, as my mum was housebound and needed things that my dad wouldn't get for her – but mostly because I loved my mum dearly and enjoyed her company.

That was until disaster struck. Like many nights, I'd call my mum and not catch her before she fell asleep. There were some nights I'd call up to 60 times trying to wake her up. Our biggest fear came true one morning – I got a call from my dad: mum had fallen out of her wheelchair and broken her leg above the knee. It was the leg she'd had the amputation. She was so frightened of what my dad would say, she spent half the night on the floor in agony until he came down in the morning. My dad slept in their old room, and the living room was converted into a bedroom with an en-suite bathroom. He had no way of knowing what had happened to my mum until the morning.

It was a dark day for our family – well, my sister and me – as my dad showed little to no emotion. We couldn't go to the hospital for obvious reasons; Covid and lockdown were a nightmare. She was lucky it was a clean break and wouldn't require

surgery. She spent a couple of days in hospital before being allowed home. They bandaged her leg up and left it to heal on its
own. Although she had a prosthetic leg, she couldn't have used
it if she wanted to.

When she finally came home, we were there to make sure
she was okay. It was heartbreaking. My mum was always larger
than life, and even though she had diminished over the years,
she was losing that spark. Seeing her like that – broken, beaten,
and reduced to an almost stranger. My sister and me hugged
our mum and did our best to hold it together for her benefit. It
wasn't easy.

As the next few months passed, life seemed to get easier.
The lockdown did have its benefits. I'm sure I'm not alone, but
there is nothing worse than standing in a queue and having
some random stranger breathing in your ear – or that close they
might as well be stroking your bottom, and without asking you
out for dinner first. Shame on them. It wasn't all bad. During
lockdown, I started having regular chats and occasional video
chats with my good friend Linzi – the one I would make late for
work at Butlins. Her way of checking on friends, and she knew
I led a lonely life. I was grateful for that human contact, although
through the phone. There are some special people out there that
will reach out without being asked to. Those friends are the ones

you should hold close to your heart and never let go. Even if you have a falling-out, there is nothing that can't be fixed if you're willing to try!

Lightning can strike twice; several months after the first fall, my mum did it again. This time she broke her leg below the knee – between the knee and the amputation. The same leg, and again she spent the night on the floor, too afraid to wake my dad up. She could have died, and nobody would have known. The break was a bad one, and due to having so little bone below the knee, surgery was not possible. She suffered, but there was nothing that could be done.

Christmas 2020 – after years of not giving my mum the whole Christmas experience – my dad finally put their Christmas tree up. It was the first time in years since my dad made an effort for someone other than himself. It was a nice day with my sister, her daughter, my parents, and me. What we didn't know – it would be my mum's last one. That Christmas, we made it the best we could for my mum. I'm glad we did.

Chapter 53

I had no idea 2021 would be the hardest year of my life. It started like every year since 2014, missing my son, unable to celebrate Christmas or his birthday. He turned 8 that year and all I thought about was all the milestones I missed and was going to miss.

Teaching him to do his shoelaces, tell the time, to read and write and be able to read stories to him at bedtime. Kicking a football around, teaching him to swim and taking him for his first day at pre-school. The list goes on, and every one of those things I wouldn't do tore me apart. It was torture. The worst part: my family hadn't met him.

I felt so much guilt. My dad never cared that he had a grandson, but my mum loved him even though she only saw him through videos and photos. There were many nights I cried myself to sleep and hated myself. I rarely spoke about him in front of my mum, instead talking to my Butlins friends. I found it easier with them. My friend Tracy got little gifts at Christmas that would be for him one day. One year she bought some sunflower seeds called 'Little Leo'. It was so thoughtful. They were meant to be miniature sunflowers, but when they came up the following year, one was 7 foot tall with over 30 flower heads. It was amazing. I'm blessed to have friends so caring and understanding.

March 14th was Mother's Day. I visited my parents the day before, as buses didn't run where we lived on a Sunday. I treated my parents to a Chinese takeaway, a family favourite. It was a lovely day. My sister was going around on the Sunday. I stayed until late evening; my mum and I had our usual last cigarette before I left. It had been a hard few years for us all. I cherished those little moments. It had been less than two years since my mum's dad passed away. He was her last parent. My mum took it hard. I didn't know that would be the last time I'd see my mum alive.

One thing that stuck with me: my mum said, 'I never imagined that I would be the one out of the 3 kids that she would be closest to', which seemed strange at the time. I just replied saying, 'Perhaps it was the health issues that we shared,' and then I left. I called her later on in my usual goodnight chat and said Happy Mother's Day, as it was Sunday morning by then.

As I struggled with my sleep so much, I didn't call her when I woke up. As my sister was going round, I planned to call in the evening. After the first fall out of her wheelchair, my mum had carers twice a day to help her wash, dress and undress, as she couldn't manage on her own. I knew when they usually went in, so I had an idea when to call her. Unfortunately, I never got the chance.

It was just after 9:00 p.m. when my mobile started ringing. It was my sister. She didn't mess about; she said Mum had become unwell early evening and went into her bathroom. She was still in there when the carer arrived, so she went in to check on her. The door was always unlocked. She found my mum on the floor unresponsive. An ambulance was called straight away and my dad called my sister. She drove round straight away and then called me. I was in my nightwear at the time, and from what my sister told me, it didn't look good and there were already too many people there. The air ambulance had been called, but they knew there was nothing they could do and left without her.

My sister had rung off and then 10 minutes later called me back with an update. My mum's pupils had blown and she wasn't responding. They had her on oxygen and were trying to wake her up, but to no avail. Something else I shared with my mum was watching medical dramas on TV, and I knew enough that when the pupils have blown, it usually means that there is no brain activity and no coming back. My sister asked me if I wanted to go round to see her one more time. I said no! There wasn't enough room to move with so many people there. I also said I'd rather remember her as she was the night before. Maybe that was a cowardly answer.

The air ambulance crew said rushing to hospital wouldn't change the outcome. The paramedics took her in. I knew they would have to do a CT scan to check for any brain activity. Then it was just a matter of waiting for her body to shut down and her heart to stop.

First thing I did was call my mate Terry. He did his best to support me, but I could tell he was upset too. He told me to call anytime through the night if I needed to chat.

It was a horrible night, expecting my phone to ring. Monday 15th March 2021 at about 4:00 a.m., my mum slipped away to the great beyond. My dad called to tell me just after 8:00 a.m., as he thought I'd be asleep. I thanked him, and as soon as I got off the phone, I broke down like I'd never done before. After 20 minutes, I was just about able to call Terry to tell him and then had the unpleasant task of telling others, mostly through messages, as it was too hard to speak. The only blessing was that she had little to no knowledge of what was happening. It would take a long time to accept she was gone and never coming back. And then the guilt kicked in. All the things I wished I'd said or done but couldn't. She knew I loved her dearly and that would have to be enough.

Then came the questions: why, how and what caused it? Due to the backlog and the continuing issues from COVID, her post-mortem was delayed. We had to wait several weeks to find out the cause of death. We had ideas of what we thought it was, but we couldn't have been further from the truth.

There were some things we expected, like her heart being on the brink of packing up, her kidneys were in bad shape, and her arteries had calcified, which meant they were so restricted that blood flow was limited at best, which in turn put more pressure on her heart. But the kicker was something none of us could have foreseen. She had a brain tumour – cancer – the big C that everyone dreads – and it was fatal. It turned out that even if they had found it, they wouldn't have been able to operate, and it was aggressive. They worked out that she'd had two previous bleeds before a fatal catastrophic bleed that finished the job. The previous bleeds explained a lot. The final one was a double bleed that strangled the brain from functioning. It was a ticking time bomb with no escape.

My sister was the most outspoken about the cancer diagnosis, as my mum had many scans over the months prior to her death. She couldn't understand why it wasn't picked up, and I understood her frustration. My mum's GP practice had become so political in its actions that patient care was neglected.

It wouldn't have helped had we known, and it's true — ignorance is bliss. It took months to come to terms with her passing. Knowing she was no longer suffering was the one saving grace. The pain was over, and she could finally rest.

I wouldn't have managed if it wasn't for certain people. Again, my Butlins family rescued me, gave me the strength to keep going. In particular, Cheryl — from the day I told her and for the whole first year — would message or call every single day, making sure I was okay and being there at silly o'clock when I couldn't sleep. Listening to me when the tears wouldn't stop, she made sure I knew I wasn't alone. She saved me in many ways. My love for her has only grown stronger, like a sister that I couldn't live without. She knew what it was like to suffer loss, and at a much younger age. Another very special woman.

Then there was Lorraine, even after her own loss — her husband Jason, who we all knew at Butlins. He passed away a few months before my mum; he was only 50. Our roles swung in roundabouts. After Jason passed, I was there day and night — my trouble sleeping had its benefits. She was a lot stronger than me and didn't hesitate to be there when I was struggling. But then again, that's Lorraine. Putting others first and being a matriarch in her own right, the glue that kept us all together. We are lucky to have her in our lives.

Another saviour was Tracy. Although we were unable to talk on the phone that much, we regularly exchanged messages. She and her family had been so kind and understanding when it came to my son, but she also lost her own father the year before. Like Lorraine, she was always there—even when she was suffering. A special woman with the world on her shoulders, and like many of my friends from Butlins, she is quick to rein in her own suffering to support others.

Then, of course, my best mates Phil and Terry, who had both met my mum and liked her a lot. It was harder with Phil, as he was working and had a family. He was still there with a kind message and an open ear if I needed it. I would regularly chat to Terry throughout the week—those first couple of months, the calls were almost daily and a godsend.

I cannot forget Janelle—always at the end of the phone, even if those conversations would last three hours. She had a knack for taking my mind off my own troubles. Another special woman. Considering she had lost her father a few years prior, like so many of my closest friends, she put her own grief aside to help others. I've always known I'm lucky—the friends I made at Butlins, when the chips are down, every single one of them would drop everything just to answer the phone or send you a message reminding you: you're not alone, you have friends, and you can do this!

They weren't the only ones that rallied round, but there are too many to name. They know who they are and how grateful I am for all their support that got me through the grieving. With the support from friends far and wide, it kept me sane when at home things were far from good.

Dealing with the loss, my sister and I grew closer, although we had always been relatively close growing up. After such a tragedy, we looked to each other for support, as we knew our dad wouldn't be there. This was made worse after our dad couldn't wait to get rid of our mum's belongings. He had no shame! We knew he wasn't the type to mourn, but a wife of 48 years deserved a lot better. It was heartbreaking, and nothing we said made a difference. Less than a month later, we noticed his phone kept going off — messages that he admitted were from women on dating websites.

After the post-mortem, it was time to plan the funeral. Covid wasn't as big by then but did mean we were limited in how many could attend. Had my sister not gone with my dad to the funeral directors, there probably wouldn't have been a funeral. As far as he was concerned, once you're gone, you're gone — no use doing anything. He didn't care that others wanted to say goodbye. He didn't want music or a service, but my sister made sure he didn't get his way. She picked the songs that she knew our mum loved, and we would hear those songs on the radio for weeks after. I would say, 'Okay mum, I know you're here,' and find peace from it.

Another thing we argued with our dad over was having our mum dressed in her own clothes. He refused, and it was one battle we couldn't win. Then, as we waited for her body to be released, I begged my dad to allow me to visit my mum at the funeral directors. As he didn't like to lose control, he kept refusing me the chance to say goodbye. It would take a constant battle and others' help before my dad finally relented. I needed it and knew it would be important that someone said goodbye.

The day she was due to arrive at the funeral directors, I had to wait before being allowed to go down. I wouldn't get long due to the funeral happening the following day. I took the best photo of my son and me and wrote a message on the back. I also picked up a single red rose for her. The lady at the funeral home took me to the room and left me alone. It was the first dead person I'd ever seen, and I quickly broke down. In my mind, I knew what I wanted to say, but it took a while. I wanted to overcome the guilt that had been building inside of me. I had to make peace at some point—otherwise, I would never get on with my life. I was there ten minutes before I had to leave. It was the first time since I was a teenager that I'd seen my mum at peace, without pain. She looked like an angel, and I knew she was going to a better place. I got to tell her best friend she looked at peace, and it was what she needed to hear. It was hard, but I am glad I did it.

I didn't sleep well that night, and the next day I wasn't at my best for the funeral. It was well out of town, and I had to go with my mum's neighbour; we sat together in the chapel. The service itself was about what you'd expect. There were plenty of tears, but I never shed any—I'd done that when I visited her the day before. One thing that was different: my dad insisted that the curtain be closed throughout the service so nobody could see her coffin.

Once it was all said and done, there was a light gathering outside in the car park, as there was no wake planned. There was no way to talk to those who'd been able to go. I got to speak to her best friend, and although brief, it was a nice moment on a sobering day. Then it was time to leave and head home. Having no gathering after spoiled it for my sister and me. Not that we wanted a big knees-up at some club, but she deserved a good send-off. She had touched so many people throughout her life, even though she only reached the age of 66.

My sister and I went back to the funeral directors to collect our mum's ashes a few days later. We wanted to keep her with us; our dad didn't want them. I had hoped I would get to see my mum again as a ghost. A couple of years prior to my mum passing, I saw my first ghost. I was in the kitchen — the light was on — and as I turned around, there stood my godmother: full apparition. I felt no fear, no shock, but seeing her standing there smiling at me just filled me with love. I blinked, and she was gone. I'd had many ghostly experiences through my lifetime, but I'd never seen an actual ghost until that day. I hoped that my mum would do the same, but so far that hasn't happened. I've seen things out of the corner of my eye that couldn't be explained. Maybe I'm not ready to see her yet — who knows?

Chapter 54

The next few months were a series of ups and downs and another loss; my mum's neighbour lost his battle to cancer in the September. There was a chance for me to finally put the guilt behind me that had been consuming me — the guilt that my mum never met her grandson in person. I knew it wasn't all my fault and a lot of the blame was down to my ex, but regardless, I should have done more. I made the mistake in believing my ex was going to be fair; I was the fool for not taking control from the day he was born. But we cannot change the past — it's what we do with the days ahead that matters.

Due to the 2020 COVID restrictions, Lorraine was unable to have a celebration of life for her husband, Jason. She decided to have it in Bognor Regis on the 1st anniversary, as that is where they met and married. I was invited and was looking forward to seeing old friends I hadn't seen for 20 years. Although the get-together was in part to mourn another loss, it was more about celebrating the life of a wonderful person who was the life and soul of the party. What better way than with some of the old Butlins team?

As I hadn't been away for 5 years, I decided to make the most of my time and booked 6 nights. I used the same B&B when I went to Terry's 40th birthday, as it was the cheapest and a nice place. Terry and his family had moved into a bigger home — a house rather than a flat. The B&B was nearer to them than the seafront, so it made visiting them easier.

I got there on the Friday and, although I was worn out from the travelling, I popped round to see Terry and his family. Being the end of November, the weather was chilly and only just above freezing. It was nice to reach their place and have a cup of coffee. It was a nice evening, and they invited me for Sunday dinner. It would be the first time that someone had cooked for me since 2012. I'd always been funny about eating at other people's homes because of my food restrictions and wouldn't want to upset anyone for being unable to eat the meal. I trusted Terry and his partner, Nic; I knew I could let them know what I can and can't eat.

That night I slept well and by Saturday morning I was ready to hit the town and the pier. I had made a pact with myself to let go of that guilt! The only way I knew how was to face my fear of walking to the end of the pier. It wasn't a long pier, but I still had that fear of walking on unsteady floors, ladders, etc. The pier was a demon I was ready to face. Saturday was the first day, and I knew I wouldn't make it to the end, but I did get over half-way. I then stood there as the wind blew through my hair and closed my eyes, just breathing in and out slowly. I did that for 20 minutes and, like the changing of the seasons, I felt the warmth of peace start to wash over me. It was revitalising; I felt lighter — I was in the right place to make peace.

Sunday — it was nice to sit down and be waited on, not something I was used to. Just being with friends and chatting made for a nice change. The whole afternoon was fun, and dinner was perfect. I rarely cook a Sunday roast; it made a nice change. I couldn't have asked for a better day. I ended up staying until evening. It was while I was there that it started to snow — something that rarely happens in Bognor Regis. It was nice walking through it back to the B&B.

Monday morning, I was up early and was ready for a chilled-out day. Those coming down for Lorraine were due that day. Then I got a phone call — Terry told me he had COVID. As it was before you could buy tests in the shops, I had no way of testing myself until I got home. As I'd been so close to him, there was a chance that I could have it too. It was hard weighing up the pros and cons about what to do. In the end, I decided there was nothing I could do. I'd had the first COVID injection — I had to trust that I would be fine.

I still managed to get down to the seafront and walked a little further along the pier. I felt I had the confidence I'd been missing for many years. It was surreal walking along the promenade and seeing snow on the beach — mind you, it was only a light dusting.

As I was making my way back to the B&B, I got a random phone call — it was my old friend Darren. He was in Bognor and nobody knew he was coming. It had been 20 years since I'd last seen him, and we agreed to meet the following morning. The week was getting interesting.

I started to feel a bit under the weather. I hoped it wasn't COVID, but my symptoms were not like COVID symptoms. Being out in the cold every day, although wrapped up warm, was taking its toll. I had the chills and just felt run down. Thankfully, the excitement of seeing my friends kept me going.

Tuesday, I woke up early again — my chills were not helped with the ensuite bathroom being cold. I didn't get time to go to the pier before I met Darren. It was an awkward greeting due to COVID, keeping our distance where possible. In the end, it was the old elbow-to-elbow bump. We wandered through town before going to the café where we were to meet other Butlins friends. Having David, Darren, Tony, and me together for the first time in 20 years was amazing. We were the main birthday shouters! Very rarely did someone else do them. Lorraine took a photo of us together — our first one — it was a special moment. We had a good crowd of us; none of us were immune to why we were there, but it couldn't be a celebration of life if we were miserable.

I'd skipped breakfast at the B&B so I could eat with everyone else, although all I had was toast. It was more like warm bread, but it didn't bother me, as I was there for the company.

After that, Darren agreed to come with me to the pier, and we reminisced and shared our memories. We then walked along the promenade to Butlins. We agreed we missed how it used to look before the hotels were built. I know change can be good and people's attitudes change — doesn't mean we have to like it.

The day flew by, and we decided to part ways so that we could freshen up for the evening. I'd been growing a beard for a few weeks, and after seeing some of the photos from earlier, I felt I looked more like a hobo. I decided it was time to shave it off. I felt much better afterwards — I hated the itching.

We met in the Wetherspoon in town. It took a while for those to notice that I'd shaved. I got to see other Butlins friends, including one of the guests, Christina — we have remained good friends for many years. There were some others there too, and I got to meet Jason's family. I could easily tell they were related. It was a great atmosphere; nobody would have known that we were gathering to say goodbye to an old friend.

We were there for an hour before we headed to the pier. Lorraine had gotten permission to spread Jason's ashes there. It was high tide, with very little light. The sea could be heard as it washed over the pebbled beach. It was a little choppy and the wind had picked up. As there were over 20 of us in a close-knit group, we created our own warmth. As the ashes were released, there was a cheer. I didn't see a single tear; Jason would have been laughing at everyone shivering on a cold winter's night.

After that, it was time for the festivities to kick up a notch — we headed to the social club near the train station. Due to not feeling 100% and partly because I didn't want to drink, I stuck to soft drinks. There was karaoke, and I'm sure a few were expecting me to sing, but I didn't want to. I hadn't sung in public for many years and was happy to watch everyone else.

I did end up having a rum and coke, as Lorraine wanted us to raise a glass and truly celebrate Jason — not just for his life, but for being one in a million. After another hour, the night was coming to a close. A few people decided to move to a pub in town that was nearer to the beach, but I was drained, and the tiredness was catching up with me, so I called it a night.

Wednesday — I had made plans to meet up with a couple of the guys in town after I'd had my usual walk to the pier. It was empty on the pier, so I felt free to talk aloud to my mum. I opened up my heart and soul, telling her all the things I wanted her to know and that I loved her so much. It was almost a mantra — all part of my way of making peace with myself as much as the decisions I had made. I believed I was close to being free of guilt — well, that guilt. Some things you can never escape, no matter how hard you try — but you do learn to accept it.

I met Darren in town and we decided to go to the cinema to watch *Ghostbusters Afterlife*. As the cinema was not a chain cinema, the tickets were much cheaper. The film was brilliant and I'm not ashamed to admit I had tears at the end. Darren looked at me and laughed. You have to watch the first two 80's movies and *Afterlife* to understand.

Afterwards, we went to the Wetherspoon for dinner — burger and chips, not very original but a cheap meal. It was the first time I'd eaten out for many years. It was quiet in the pub and the food was much better than my hometown Wetherspoon. I knew when I got home that I would need to eat much better after a poor diet. Mind you, I was getting too old to worry too much about my waistline. My metabolism had long since slowed down and exercising was far from easy when you are disabled. Then again, I had a plan to tackle that the following year.

Thursday morning, it was time to have a nice cooked breakfast before heading home. I had enough time for one more trip to the pier. I finally found peace! I achieved what I set out to do and I felt like I could finally start moving on with my life. I wasn't completely free, but you have to start somewhere. Farewell, Bognor — I will see you again.

Chapter 55

I got home safe and sound but felt rough. I'd ordered a Covid test that was waiting for me when I got home. It was agonising waiting for the results, but I got the all-clear. I was relieved and quickly told Terry, as he was worried he'd passed it to me. It ended up being a bad cold that lasted throughout December and into the New Year. I was so bad, my sister and dad had to come to mine on Christmas Day to exchange gifts. I barely left the house for five weeks. I rarely got ill, but when I did, it usually lasts.

It was January 2022 that I made a decision about my weight. I knew I couldn't afford to go to the gym and certainly didn't have the energy to go that far. I saved some money, and with the help of vouchers, I treated myself to an exercise bike. I knew I was being brave, as technically I'm not meant to cycle, but was desperate to try something.

A couple of years earlier, on my annual health review, they found I had high blood pressure that was bad enough to warrant blood pressure tablets. I was just over 40 by then, and they told me the usual 'it's because of your age', as though that's the answer to most of my health problems. I couldn't take the chance they were wrong; it seemed my whole life revolved around taking one tablet or another.

When the exercise bike arrived, I was apprehensive. My knees were awful but had to try. I started by doing a 15-minute session in the morning and then a half-hour session in the evening. It took a couple of weeks to get a rhythm going. Some days I only managed 10 minutes in the morning and 20 minutes in the evening, but I was determined to keep going.

After six weeks, I started pushing for longer and was pleased to see the weight coming off. It was slow at first, but once I started doing 30 minutes in the morning and an hour in the evening, the results spoke for themselves. After three months, I'd lost half a stone. This may seem trivial to some, but to me, it was massive. For five and a half years, I'd done everything I possibly could to lose the weight I'd gained after the bunion operation. My willpower was a lot stronger than I realised, and by the time I'd been using the bike for nine months, I'd lost a stone. I couldn't believe it. It was just a start and I still weighed more than I would have liked. I'd also been using some light weights for upper body strengthening. I'd been doing them a couple of years; the progress was slow but was starting to show.

Then August came, and another funeral — this time it was Christina's mum. Christina and her parents were regulars at

Butlins. Although it was inevitable, it was still hard for her family and those who knew her. It was one of the hottest days of the year, and wearing a shirt, tie, and trousers was not ideal. Lorraine was also close to the family, so we met at the train station in London where the service was being held. You could see by all the mourners how many lives she had touched, and she got a good send-off. What made the day more memorable — I went without any crutches for the first time in ten years. I was proud of myself, even if I had to wear knee supports. By the time I got home, I was a mess — it took several days before I recovered.

As September arrived, I had something to look forward to. Janelle had twisted my arm and persuaded me to go back to Butlins for another holiday. Like I needed persuading. We stayed in a different hotel this time, the one that backed on to Hotham Park. We dipped in with the weather, as it was still warm with mostly cloudless blue skies. After a turbulent few months, the break was well needed, as was the company. As an added bonus, Lorraine had moved back to Bognor and had planned to get together one evening.

Although it was mid-September, Butlins was still busy enough. There was a very attractive lady we saw on the first evening out, and Janelle asked me if I'd spotted her, to which I replied, 'The one with the long red dress and very attractive?

No, I hadn't.' It was quite funny at the time. Over the next three days, everywhere we went, that same woman would appear — it definitely gave us something to laugh about.

We made sure we saw some of the entertainment, as there were some good acts on. It made a change to sit back as a holidaymaker rather than an ex-member of staff. After losing so much weight and strengthening my body, I felt more confident than I had in years — and what better place to test that out than Butlins? It showed, as I started chatting with a lady and we got on well. It was nice to feel like a man again.

The biggest achievement came when Janelle and me popped round to see Lorraine and David, as they were living together. I decided to go out without any crutches. I was nervous after years being dependent on them. Using knee supports and having Janelle close by gave me confidence. We arrived mid-afternoon, and Lorraine had done some snacks and made drinks for us. David is more laid-back, but they both welcomed us to their home. Lorraine's dog was funny, way too much energy, and always wanted a fuss. It was a nice afternoon, and we even had a video chat with a couple of other Butlins friends. It was difficult fitting four people into a mobile phone screen. I was glad we got some quality time with friends. When I was younger, it was easy to not appreciate your friends and take them for granted.

That day without crutches, I felt like a man again. Women didn't look at me as a disabled man, though I still lacked the confidence to chat to women properly. I paid for my braveness for days afterwards. While we had a couple more days left at Butlins, we took it slower. I told myself to just make it through the next couple of days and then I could rest once home. Don't get me wrong, I loved being at Butlins, but it's expensive and not the kind of place you can easily relax. We made the most of our time; four nights quickly came to a close, and it was time to leave. Once we were off-site and made our way to the train station, we said our goodbyes and promised to message when we were home safe.

Once I was home and in my flat, I locked the door, dumped my belongings, and crashed out for the next few days. I couldn't believe how brave I'd been—not just going without crutches, but doing more than normal. The whole week had been a wake-up call to what was possible. I knew I'd slip into the old routine—going days without seeing or talking to anyone. Only going out for shopping or visiting family. It was a lonely life, but it was my life! There were those rare moments when I felt well enough to do a little bit more, but most of the time I'd be fighting to get the housework done or build myself up to do gardening. Daily battles I couldn't escape—but it still meant I was alive. I had a long way to go to reach my dream of moving back to Bognor, to be nearer to my friends and finally see my son again.

The next couple of months seemed to fly by; just like that, another Christmas had arrived. Another time for celebration — well, for everyone else. I didn't bother doing anything for New Year's Eve; most nights I was in my loungewear before it was even dark. I certainly didn't bother with watching TV — I stuck to DVDs. To me, every 'big' day is just that — another day not to get excited about. I always dreaded Father's Day; it felt like a joke at my expense. I got one Father's Day, but every year after that just got harder and harder. Even the few drinks I had over the festive period did nothing to dull the pain.

I figured that 2023 would be another long-winded, dull year. I was wrong for a change. The first month was depressing until I made a decision. My son was going to be 10. I decided to get something special for his birthday. My mum didn't understand why I continued to buy presents for my son, as he would grow out of most of it by the time I got to see him. I tried to explain it was the principle, and I didn't know if I'd be in a position to see him that year. I'd say that every year — live in hope. It's hard to know what to buy when you don't know what your kid likes. I wanted to buy things that I would have liked and hope that he really is my mini-me. Not just looks, but likes and loves.

I still had Sky TV and, with it, the Sky VIP app. I tried many of the competitions that came up. I'd already won a couple of things that I was unable to use, like tickets to the Newmarket Nights live event. It was to see Irish group The Script, but I was too unwell to go. I hoped for better luck.

The first win was tickets to see Pretty Woman: The Musical. Yes, the most manly musical possible. I asked my friend if he fancied going, and he said yes. I don't think he realised what he was accepting. I'd been to the theatre once, when I saw Les Misérables with school, and I loved it. I've wanted to see others, but for one reason or another, it never happened.

I was the one with egg on my face when he suggested doing some London sightseeing. It wasn't a case of "let's go to the Natural History Museum and spend a few hours in the area." Oh no—he dragged me on and off tube trains like a yo-yo: Marble Arch, the pub where the Krays once killed someone, the Strand, and the palace where the King was for a few days before his coronation. The show was in the West End at the Savoy Theatre — couldn't have chosen a more posh place. I was dressed in jeans and a T-shirt. It was a hot day, and I was sweating and shattered; no amount of deodorant could mask the smell.

I did get to meet my good friend Nicolas. He lived and worked in London, and we hadn't seen each other in 20 years. We arranged to meet near where he worked for a catch-up. It made the day more special. Although the time we had together was short, it was well worth all the tube-hopping we'd done.

When we went into the theatre, I stocked up on drink, then found our seats in the poshest place I'd ever been. It wasn't until I had a good look round that I realised we were an abnormality. It was mostly couples or groups of the same sex — except we were the only two straight guys together. I knew it was going to be a great crowd. The show didn't disappoint; it was amazing, and by the end, there was a standing ovation. My mate loved it too — we both joined in with the clapping. We were buzzing when we left.

We had planned to eat in London, but never seemed to find the time or a place that appealed, so grabbed a McDonald's on the way home. I paid for being on my feet so long and all the stairs. I stumbled up and down most of them. Once I got home, it was 1:00 a.m. I just about managed my tablets before going to bed. I slept 12 hours straight. It took me nearly a week to recover.

There were a couple of quiet months before I got a welcome visitor. My friend Phil had a free weekend and asked if I fancied some company. I hadn't seen him since his wedding in 2014 — it was nice to make up for lost time. It was July, and the weather was dreadful; it rained most of the time. Ironically, it was similar to the weather when we went to Corfu. We did go out a couple of times, including to the cinema, but mostly sat around my flat chatting and watching movies. It was nice to relax and have company — a rarity nowadays. There is something about my Butlins friends that makes your life better.

The next big win came in August. It was the Heritage Live event at Audley End House near Saffron Walden. The last concert I went to was Alanis Morissette in 1998, so I was excited at seeing live music again. The acts were Toploader, The Feeling, Embrace, and the headliners were Razorlight. I'd heard of them all except Embrace — mind you, Toploader I only knew the one song that I'm sure everybody knows, and The Feeling I knew were great. I was blown away with it all. It was a mostly overcast day with a breeze and not too hot — until the clouds broke and the sun shone through.

Toploader were first. They were very good and engaged with the crowd well. Next were The Feeling — they were hilarious with brilliant music, some songs I knew. Then came Embrace. I didn't know any of their songs, but I was blown away. One song that stuck with me the most was Ashes. I was so moved by their music that the day after the concert, I went straight on Amazon and ordered the first couple of albums on CD. I now have all of their albums. When Razorlight came on, I was disappointed. I only knew a couple of songs, and the rest I didn't like much, plus the lead singer was unpleasant. He looked like he was either high or just a crazy person. It didn't help that there was a couple standing in front of us jumping around and swinging their arms. It got so bad I nearly got knocked over several times. That, and they were practically screaming the words — fortunately, I wasn't wearing my hearing aids.

Considering it only cost me £10 for the parking and then the drinks, it was a brilliant afternoon/evening and we both had a fantastic day. One thing I would say — for those like me who grew up with indie or Britpop — if you get the chance to see Embrace, do it, you won't be disappointed. After the show, we waited until everyone left so the traffic was lighter, and ended up having to leave the back way as the front gates were closed. We were both shattered by the time we got home. Although it took a great deal out of us, the combination of adrenaline and sheer willpower kept us going. Once back in my flat, it hit like a tidal wave. Once again, I slept for 12 hours. Sometimes I think I'm getting too old to have fun.

Since my mum passed, I'd grown closer to my mum's best friend. Although the cancer was taking its toll on her, she was still happy to video chat each week. We could talk for hours about anything and everything. But then, late autumn, she succumbed and joined my mum on the other side. It had become a devastating two years of people I knew passing. This was a lot closer to home. Her funeral was beautiful and filled with lots of laughs. I understood why she and my mum got on so well — they made life better for being in it.

Since the start of COVID, I had seen my mum, her best friend, her neighbour — all from cancer. Then three members of staff I worked with at Butlins — the youngest was only 40 — and then there were three parents of people I knew through Butlins. It was far too many. I realised how important it was to keep going and fighting, as tomorrow is not guaranteed.

Chapter 56

Don't worry, we are near the end!For years I contemplated my own mortality and what the future may or may not hold, especially when it came to my son. I have this fear that I wouldn't live long enough to get things sorted with him. Or knowing the family he hadn't met, as well as telling him the truth about why I wasn't there. I doubt anyone around him would say a good word about me. Would he even believe me if I sat him down and told him the truth from my perspective? So many thoughts and concerns that would drive me crazy every day. I knew I had to do something in case the worst does happen.

I decided to write to him, write a long letter explaining how I first met his mum back in 2002 and the whirlwind romance that abruptly ended and then restarted 10 years later. One of the hardest parts: explaining why I wasn't at his birth. I knew it would be hard. I would have to dig deep into my heart and pull out the memories, good and bad. Telling him I loved his mum and always would, to some degree. How it took me 20 years before I stopped loving her. I know I did wrong and was far from innocent, but my actions were with his best interest at heart. I hated leaving his mum, but if I'd stayed, I probably wouldn't have lived long enough to see him born.

The more I wrote, the more the tears came and the more my heart was crushed. I hated myself for letting him down. I would have done anything and everything I could to be the best father for him. What should have taken a week or two ended up taking over two months. There was a lot of stop, start and questioning myself. Was I doing the right thing? Was I coming across as a horrible, bitter person or as a loving father who made mistakes? Would he ever forgive me? So many questions and no answers!

I'd nearly finished the letter as Christmas arrived. I'm not a big drinker, but that year I needed something to help me mentally and emotionally cope. It took a lot out of me and left a void in my heart. I'd started to lose my way again; I knew things had to change.

It took a few weeks until I finally pulled myself back from the edge. 2024 was here, and I needed to start moving forwards. My emotional state had improved; my physical state was in tatters. Aches and pains I'd endured for years had become so bad it was unbearable. I struggled to do as much as I used to. I still kept up the exercise bike, but found it hard to maintain the same rhythm. Wearing knee supports was a daily necessity, even when indoors.

It was frustrating. After years and years of battling the pain, my knees would regularly give way on me. No matter how hard you try to stay on your feet and maintain a semblance of normal life, it felt like the world was against you. But that's just a normal day when you're disabled, living alone and unable to work. Every day is a battle that nobody can see; we persevere because we have to. Those days you're confined to the sofa, you either go hungry or suffer unimaginable pain just to do some toast. But when we do go out, we smile and laugh and pretend that everything is fine, when deep down you just want to crawl into a corner and cry.

I used to go out with my real face, the one that showed how much I was truly suffering. I'd get stopped and asked what was wrong. I tried to be polite and say I'm fine, but some people were persistent. I'd eventually give them the shortened version; it didn't go down well. Their mouth would drop, their eyes would widen and then shake their head. You could tell they wished they'd never asked. I got fed up of having to explain myself, so I'd put on a fake smile. I hated myself for being a fraud. I decided it was better to be a fraud than have strangers make out they cared when in reality most didn't. Well, maybe that's a bit harsh — more like they wish they didn't hear it, as it made them uncomfortable. Some people live in their own bubble, happily oblivious to others' suffering.

You are probably wondering why I said "we" — well, it's simple! I'm not alone suffering a daily battle with my own body. Many are better off than me, and some much worse. I saw the way my mum suffered and the way I've suffered. Most of my friends are lucky by having a partner and a family for support. They give them purpose to fight. Yes, I'm a father, and wanting to see him and be with him is my light in the dark.

July and August, I pushed myself and did much more than normal. It was my friend Terry's stag do and wedding. The stag do was an eye-opener. We went for a round of football golf — yes, that really is a thing. It was a 12-hole course with bigger holes near the golfing holes, and we had a football instead of a golf ball. There were four of us altogether, which worked out well. I quickly learnt I was far too old to be kicking a football, especially footballs made of lead — at least they felt like they were. It was harder being a hot summer's day.

We then did an escape room; this was something only Terry's son had done, like the football golf. We ended up with the hardest room. It was definitely an experience; we failed miserably but had a good laugh. At least we escaped the scorching sun for a little while.

We went for a meal at a Smith & Western restaurant. Again, something of a revelation for me, as I hadn't eaten at a restaurant in years. It was very much as it sounded — an American-style restaurant where the staff were dressed as cowboys and cowgirls. The meal was perfect, the company was better and the laughs were contagious. It was a brilliant day and night for a dear friend. We didn't need a nightclub or lots of drink, just good company. We finished the night in the pub we were staying at and played poker — yeah, I lost at that too.

Five weeks later was the wedding. I'd booked for five nights; I was excited, as I planned to catch up with friends while I was there. I arrived in Bognor on the Thursday afternoon. It was very wet and very windy. I made it to the B&B in one piece — albeit soggy. It was a new B&B, as my usual one had closed. I was gutted, as it was a lovely place and much cheaper. The new one was much closer to the beach, so had that going for it.

Due to the weather and the fact I was worn out, I called for a taxi to take me to Terry's home. I'd agreed to pop round, as I didn't know when we'd get the chance to meet up. I'd been there an hour when they had visitors. It was Terry's friend Ross from America and his wife. Although they often spoke, it was the first time they'd met in person. I was excited to meet the man I'd heard so much about. Ross was everything I'd heard about and so much more. We would soon become good friends too.

I stayed a little while longer, but as it was starting to get crowded and, being worn out, I made my apologies and left. I decided to walk back to the B&B, and even though I had done the journey by foot before, I decided to take a detour. I screwed up. Yes, you guessed it—another lesson learnt. I would end up walking nearly a mile out of my way. By the time I got back to the B&B, I was soaked, shattered and embarrassed.

The next morning, I woke feeling refreshed and excited for a busy day. The weather was much better. My spirits were dampened when I started itching. It was after checking the bed that I found bed bugs. Bugger! It was my second day, and I was due to stay there for another four nights—decisions, decisions. I told the cleaner and showed her what I'd found. She was shocked and quickly went to change the bed covers. It was later that day, after a little research, I found out changing the covers wasn't enough—they would need to fumigate the room.

I decided to make the most of the lovely day and took a long stroll along the promenade. I passed Butlins and went as far as Felpham. I'd reached my special spot and just stood there, taking it all in. I was glad it was quiet, as I was lost in thought and didn't want to be disturbed. It was nice and peaceful; all the old memories came flooding back, and I had to smile.

I was in contact with my friend Tracy. We'd been trying to meet up for years but it never seemed to happen. This time, she and her family were going to make it for our first catch-up in nine years. When we saw each other, we both smiled — there were big hugs. A handshake with her husband and a hug from both her sons. Her youngest is only six months younger than my son.

We went to Hatters, the Wetherspoons. We all had soft drinks except Tracy. Her husband suggested getting Tracy alcohol — of course, we got a double. We stayed there for an hour, and by then Tracy had polished off two double Jack Daniels and Coke. The effect was obvious. It was hilarious. I'd learnt that Tracy can be very chatty, but when alcohol is involved, she could talk for England.

We then headed to the beach for a dip in the sea. It was high tide, so didn't have to walk far. The fun begun when her youngest son, being so excited, practically jumped into the sea. It was a fun afternoon with lots of laughter. We got plenty of photos, but sadly our time together was short. We had hugs all round before having to say farewell.

After spending a little time in my room, I headed back out to see Lorraine, who worked a short walk from the B&B. We chatted for a while before I went round to her home to see David. After catching up, we headed out to meet Lorraine and walk her home.

After leaving their home, I remembered the bug problem. That would be the least of my problems. When I turned on the tap, I found there was little to no water. I messaged the owners. I was told they had no water, and the plumber couldn't get there until 8.00 a.m. – just what I needed when I had to shower early. I couldn't do much about the water and had the worst shave of my life.

I spent the night on the toilet seat trying to sleep, as it was the furthest I could get from the bed. It was one of the worst nights at the worst possible time. The plumber was there on time but had to wait until half nine before he turned the water on so I could shower. The water was a trickle. I was glad I wasn't going back after the wedding. The weather had taken a turn and rained heavily. I was smart enough to buy an umbrella the day before, so didn't ruin my suit. Through all the trials and tribulations, I finally got done and was ready for the taxi to take me to the wedding venue.

Terry and Nic had arranged a room for me at the hotel where the wedding was. It was the poshest place I'd ever been in, let alone stayed at. It was overwhelming at first, but everyone was polite. Once I got settled, I got to enjoy the day. I've known Terry for 24 years, and it was the first time I'd seen him in a suit—mind you, it was the first time he'd seen me in one.

A week before the big day, Terry asked if I would be his witness. I said yes. It was the greatest honour I'd ever had. This meant I got to sit on the front row with the best men. I managed to avoid using a crutch for the service—wearing knee supports on both knees made it possible. I'd had the maximum medicine I could have and left the crutch back in my room. I felt like a man again. It's amazing the difference leaving your walking aid can do to your confidence.

We all stood as Nic made her way down the aisle. She looked stunning. Terry was in awe; you could see the emotion flowing from them both. It was a culmination of many years together and a dream to marry. Terry was struggling to find his words as they said their vows. I'd never seen him so vulnerable and full of emotion—it was enough to make us all choke up. It was a beautiful moment. I was so happy to see them finally realise their dream. I doubt it could have gone any better, and just like that, they were husband and wife. Then came our roles as witnesses to sign the paperwork. I was shaking and only just managed to write my signature.

Once we left the room where the wedding was, it was time for a much-needed cigarette. The bride and groom had the fun of their photos being taken. The weather wasn't very nice but brightened up later on. The rest of us went to the bar and got a head start on the drinking. I started the cider rush; I had a pint of Aspall Cider and others saw it and thought they would try it.

Then came the meal. It was my first posh dinner, and by the time we started to eat, I was on my third pint — not my smartest move. I had soup for starters, which was nice until the butter in the middle melted and I couldn't eat it anymore — my problem with dairy products again a problem. The main course was much nicer: shin beef and potato, which was very nice. Although I'd hardly eaten in days, I couldn't eat it all. Dessert was a dairy-free vanilla ice cream with strawberries. I'd never had dairy-free anything before; it wasn't bad.

Once dinner was cleared, the speeches followed. Ross thought Terry and Nic were joking when they told him he was going first. But, as far as speeches go, he nailed it — which left the other best man admitting he couldn't beat it. After they were finished, the surprises started. Gifts were handed out, and that included one for me. I was shocked but grateful — a bottle of rum, my favourite.

Thankfully, the rain stopped once we'd finished eating. Most of us spent the rest of the day outside in the smoking area. Once the sun made an appearance, it was warm enough to enjoy the outside. By this time, I was struggling, so had to go back to my room and grab my crutch for the rest of the day.

I would end up spending most of my time with Ross and his wife; our friendship was quickly cemented. I'd gone on to drinking soft drinks as I didn't want to get drunk — those days are long behind me. It was a beautiful service and a perfect day with great people. I was so glad they got the day they deserved. By bedtime, I was well and truly shattered.

The next morning, I was up early and met a few others at the breakfast station. Everyone planned to meet at the same time, but being early meant I got first dibs on the coffee, which was amazing. It soon got busy.

Most people left after breakfast, but I stayed longer. Being quieter, it was easier to talk to Terry and Nic. It was nice seeing them so relaxed and full of love. The sun was shining on and off with some clouds. Knowing I had a long journey home, I decided to catch the train after midday. This would be my downfall.

One of Terry's friends was kind enough to offer me a lift to the station; I was ready to get home to my own bed. I was gutted I didn't get the other two nights in Bognor, but without an instant refund, I didn't have the money for another B&B. I was confident I would get home at a decent time — the travel gods had it in for me that day.

Once on the train to London, I checked I could change at Three Bridges so I didn't need to use the London Underground. This is what I'd usually do when travelling to and from Bognor to Cambridge. Sundays it didn't, which meant I had no choice but to use the Underground.

When you have a suitcase, any travel through London is difficult, but when you're disabled, it's a whole different kind of hell. The majority of people are so focused on what they are doing, they have no consideration for others around them. To make matters worse, the lifts I needed were some distance from the platforms — not ideal when you suffer anxiety, especially in crowded places.

Somehow I made it to Tottenham Hale station, as that was the only one with trains to Cambridge. I got there just after 3.00

p.m., and it was rammed. That was when those gates of hell opened on the whole station. First came the notice that various trains had been cancelled. This was followed by lots of people standing around in confusion. There was a broken rail on the route to Cambridge, stopping all travel — including the trains to Stansted Airport. I was stuck!

Once I'd been waiting three hours, I was in panic mode. I laid out my frustration on Facebook. This was the smartest thing I'd done that day. Forty-five minutes later, I got a message from my neighbour. This was followed by a phone call that would save me more stress and anxiety. My neighbour offered to pick me up. After taking a detour to a train station just outside London, my neighbour arrived not long after. I was so relieved the nightmare was finally over. I'd spent four hours waiting for a train that would never arrive. I was so relieved to be home — until I realised I had a suitcase to clean. Last thing I needed was bedbugs following me home.

It may have ended badly, but I did have some amazing moments. I caught up with friends, saw my best mate fulfil his dream, and made some new friends whilst dealing with some of the worst luck. The icing on the cake — I managed to lose 3 lbs in three nights, although I put it back on a week later.

As of September 2024, I have been without a partner for over 10 years — that's a decade without even kissing a woman. Those who knew me at Butlins would probably think, 'It can't be possible, not Goody.' Sadly, it is all true. Everything I have written in this book is true. Some dates may be out of order, but still completely true. I've been maybe a little too honest, but better that than lying.

For the last eight years, I've been living in my flat. Apart from three separate days when I asked for help, everything else I've done on my own. This includes the gardening, housework, cooking, DIY and everything in between. I'm proud of that. It hasn't been easy, and there have been days I have been in so much pain I've cried my heart out because I can't cope with it. It never gets any easier. You learn what you can and can't do, and some days you push yourself regardless of how long it will take to recover. At 45, I like to think I have a lot of years left in me and intend to make something of the time I have left — a lasting legacy, friendships, love and a family. All things I long to achieve, and although it has taken me a lot longer than I hoped for most things, I'm still hopeful my time will come.

The hardest part is being on my own. I'm not talking about sex. Don't get me wrong, we all have urges and needs, but it's more simple than that. It's the cuddles, someone to share a meal with, waking up next to someone and that first kiss of the day. Then it's the cuddled up on the sofa, watching a movie and eating rubbish. The days out just for the sake of it, and the holidays that I've never really had. When you get down to the nitty-gritty, I am a simple man and easily pleased. I've waited a very long time to meet someone that sees me for me, that loves me for me, who cares about me and not just themselves.

I came close to this with Karen back at Butlins and blew it — and lost a friend as well as a partner. But since part 1 of this book came out, we have cleared the air and truths that were hidden by supposed friends have come to light, and we can now talk freely.

All those years lost because the waters were muddied. I have learnt a lot about myself and what I can handle — usually the hard way. I didn't do it alone; I was never without support and always had somebody at the end of the phone. My life story has definitely been eventful, and if you are reading this, then I truly hope it helps you in your own life. I hope my mistakes can be used as warning signs that save you from losing someone you love — save you from thinking there is no way out other than the grave. I'm very lucky that a job at Butlins gave me so much, and this is me giving something back. Thank you for your patience in reading this, and good luck with whatever future you decide.

Cheryl, Terry, Janelle, Phil, Louise, Tracy, Christina, Lorraine — in no particular order — and many more. All in their own way, whether a random message checking in on me or responding to a cryptic or sad post on Facebook. There is always someone who will be there to back you up and support you, and we do the same in return. There is no tally or list of how many times one person or another has been in a bad place. None of it matters, because we are in it together. We are a family and share a love that surpasses any blood family. That is what Butlins is to me, and I am truly blessed to know them!

For many years, I wanted to write about my time at Butlins and about the friends I made along the way. But over the years, the idea grew and grew until it took on a life of its own. I've never written anything before. What I have done is tell it from the heart and in a way, a thank you to all those that helped me become the man I am today. To the women who showed me that you can be friends without romance, and the women that were romance first and friends after — I can only thank you for your patience and understanding, especially Karen, who taught me so much, even if I didn't appreciate you at the time. I have no excuses, but you're better off with the life you have than any I could have given you. I am blessed to know you all — to have worked with you, drunk with you, cried with you and danced with you. There are days I don't deserve you, but I will always be grateful for you.

It is easy to take for granted those closest to you without realising it — I have been there. It's easy to look back and say 'what if', or 'if only', and not appreciate the little things that really do matter the most. So, be inspired, be kind, love, learn, forgive, live, make mistakes and learn from them — and never forget where you came from. Try to remember that you are never alone in this world, and you can succeed even if you stumble along the way — you can do it if you're willing to put the work in. Life really is too short, so don't waste it on anger, regret and all the bad things that can make you bitter and resentful — it really isn't worth it. Find peace in life, and remember to breathe. Finally, understand your past — then you'll appreciate your future!

It's the end of this book, but not the end of the story. It can't be, as I am still alive. There are many chapters yet to be written. I recently reconnected with an old flame, Sam. I was 19 when we dated, and she's the only beautiful, kind, good woman I've had a relationship with in my hometown. Like I said — tomorrow isn't written yet, and anything can happen! I hope my story will

inspire others and give them strength when they feel weak —
and when struggling, you don't do it alone. Good luck, be
blessed, and find peace!

By Mathew Goody

With Thanks:

I haven't been able to mention every person that made Butlins so special, so here is my chance to do that. You are all wonderful people, and it's been an honour knowing you.

Staff: Phil, Janelle, Cheryl, Lorraine, Terry, Louise, Karen, Laura, Jayne, Graham, Michelle, Andy, Nicolas, Sophia, Lindsay, Gordon, Tony, Rachael, Angela, Paul, Nicola, Yvonne, Debbie, Sharlene, Clare, Carrie, Jason, Jo, David, Linzi, Benedicte, J.J., Cheryl, Russell, Liz, Carla, Mandy, Gwen, Sarah, Thomas, Rob, Nicholas, Darren, Emma, Kelly, Emma, Lisa, Steve, Jon, Kevin, Brian, Colin, Anne-Marie, Dawn, John, Ant, Natalie, Kelvin, Tammy, Leanne, Mharrie, Andrew, Elvis, Rob, Jo, Heather, Agnes, Alex and Hannah.

Guests: Tracy, Nina, Christina & Family, Gainah, Steph, Bev, Hayleigh, Emma, Tracy, Jasmine & Leonie.

And to all the others whose names I have forgotten: thank you for the memories and the letters – I am glad I have kept them after all these years.

For those who are no longer with us, you will never be forgotten!

GALLERY

One of the last photos with my mum.

London 2021 with my friend Ray before seeing Pretty Woman the musical.

At my mate Terry's wedding August 2024.

First time I met my son 2013.

Nicholas and me Halloween 2001

Fancy dress butlins 2001 with my manager Russell. I loved that dress.

Butlins May 2001 when they got me on my birthday.

The last time I saw my son 2013

Halloween 2001 the Addams family, best night ever.

John Lewis Christmas party 2007. The only time I've worn a tuxedo

My favourite photo with my son summer 2013

My wedding day with Phil who was best man.

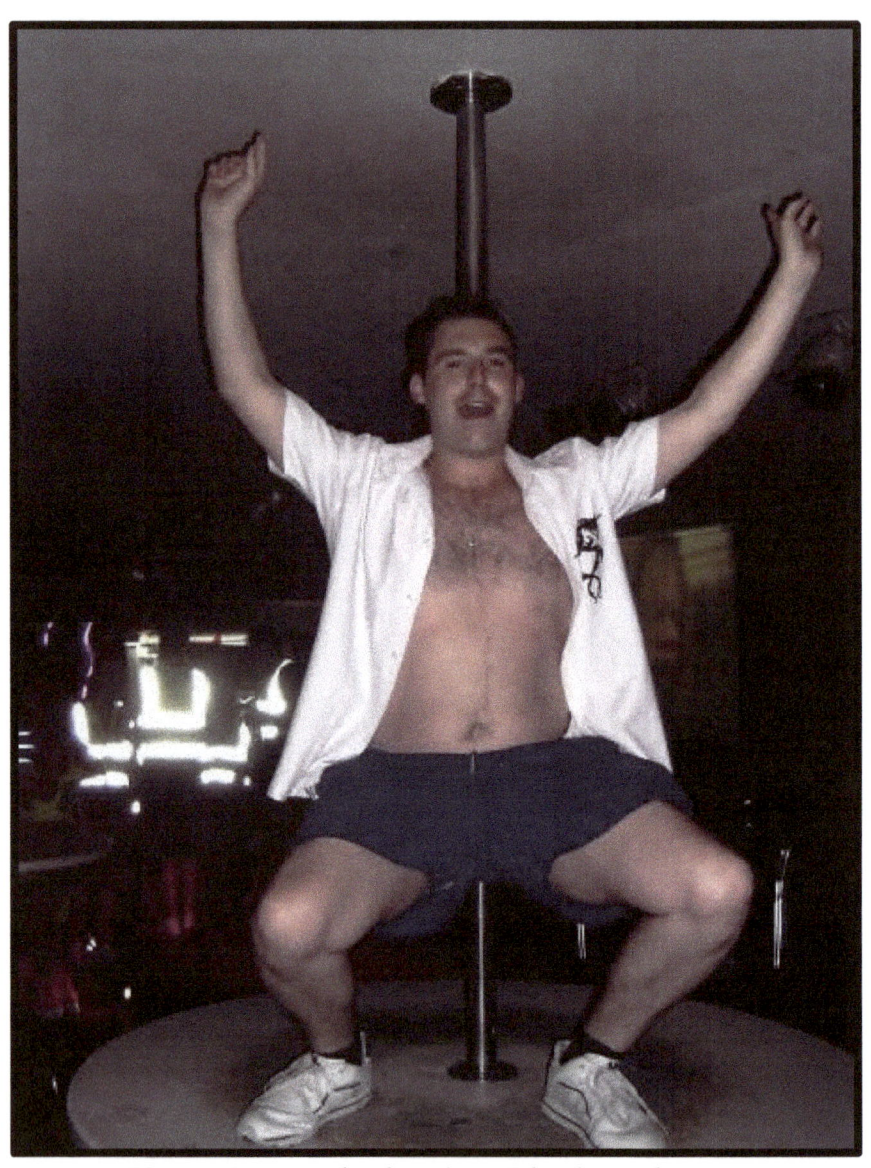

Kavos 2008 pole dancing, I had no shame.

My godmother Aunt Nan who passed when I was 7 but saw as a ghost 2018.

The day I met Tracy 1999 at butlins

Tracy and me 25 years later still close friends.

The sunset over Bognor pier, the photo that went into the local paper.

www.ingramcontent.com/pod-product-compliance
Lightning Source LLC
Chambersburg PA
CBHW051155120626
46547CB00012B/1063